MY NEXT MOVE
FORWARD

TASHA SCHUH

Karla,

Always have

hope!

Tasha

MINNEAPOLIS

ISBN 13: 978-1-63489-102-8
LCCN: 2017959397

Printed in the United States of America
First Printing: 2017
21 20 19 18 17   5 4 3 2 1

Cover design by Nupoor Gordon.
Interior Design by Patrick Maloney

Wise Ink Creative Publishing replaces every tree used in printing their books by planting thousands of trees every year in reforestation programs. Learn more at wiseinkpub.com.

Wise Ink Creative Publishing
837 Glenwood Avenue
Minneapolis, MN 55405

To Doug, for choosing to join my journey and proving what God has been telling me all along, that I am worthy to be loved.

"To love at all is to be vulnerable. Love anything and your heart will be wrung and possibly broken. If you want to make sure of keeping it intact you must give it to no one, not even an animal. Wrap it carefully round with hobbies and little luxuries; avoid all entanglements. Lock it up safe in the casket or coffin of your selfishness. But in that casket, safe, dark, motionless, airless, it will change. It will not be broken; it will become unbreakable, impenetrable, irredeemable. To love is to be vulnerable."

—C. S. Lewis, *The Four Loves*

CONTENTS

INTRODUCTION

After showcasing her talent as the lead in her high school's production of *Grease*, Tasha Schuh began to dream of a career in theater. No one knew that the stage itself would steal her dream—and almost her life—during a rehearsal for the next big show.

Just days before her opening night performance in *The Wizard of Oz*, sixteen-year-old Tasha took one step backward and fell sixteen feet through a trap door. On that day, November 11, 1997, she landed on the concrete floor of the historic Sheldon Theater, breaking her neck, crushing her spinal cord, and fracturing her skull. She would never walk again.

For the next three days, Tasha prepared for a surgery that would at best leave her a C-5 quadriplegic. Post-op complications turned Tasha's struggle and ultimate triumph into an unbelievable journey. From loss and grief to self-discovery and achievement, Tasha's faith, resilience, and honesty have allowed her to leave the old Tasha behind.

She confronted the new Tasha's life from a state-of-the-art wheelchair and faced her demons—something she called "the what-ifs." What if she had not been so passionate about theater? What if she had studied the stage directions more closely to learn everybody's task, not just her own? What if she had gone out for basketball that year? She wouldn't have been at play practice until later that night. What if she had died during that post-surgery period when infection set in and a deadly bout with septic shock almost killed her? At one point in her recovery, Tasha's temperature spiked to 108 degrees for eight days straight. She wondered, what if she had never recovered from that? What if she couldn't face life as the new Tasha Schuh?

With time and healing, Tasha began to recognize the second chance she'd been given. Admittedly struggling at first, she began to see her world with new eyes. She couldn't continue to "stuff it"—a phrase Tasha used when describing her desire to ignore the truth. Stuffing the hurt, the loss, and the frustration of adapting to a new way of life just wasn't for her.

In a quietly heroic way, Tasha picked up the pieces and set out to navigate the world of quadriplegia. With help from her family, her caregivers, and her growing faith, Tasha soon saw that she could accomplish more from a wheelchair than she ever dreamed possible in her life before disability.

Learning to let go of the what-ifs through recovery and a sincere desire for a second chance on life, Tasha attended college and earned two bachelor's degrees. She started her own business as a writer and an inspirational speaker and accomplished many other things along the way. Tasha's poignant memoir, *My Last Step Backward*, seeks to inspire readers to welcome adversity and face their own trap door of opportunity.

But something seemed off. Independence, achievements, and professional growth gave Tasha reasons to be proud. However, too often, she caught herself asking, *What is missing?*

Perhaps the better question was, *Who is missing?*

CHAPTER ONE

DUPED INTO ONLINE DATING

*C*OME ON, *PICK IT up. Who goes 55 on a highway marked 55 mph!?*

I was on a mission to get home, fast. I had to beat Rachel. I had to arrive home early enough to log on to my computer and read the latest message. But it was already twelve fifteen. Rachel—my close friend and massage therapist—was expected by twelve thirty, and I was tailgating the most law-abiding driver in Wisconsin.

I just need an extra ten minutes. Move it—pleeease?!

If I didn't beat Rachel, I'd have to wait another hour before reading his words . . . his most recent message, which was likely written in the middle of the night. I had figured out, after a few weeks of what was now a serious online relationship, that Doug Michaels replied to me long after I had gone to bed. If I could have waited up for his messages, waited until his evening shift on the air as a meteorologist ended, waited for his words to arrive at midnight or even as late as one in the morning—*This guy's a night owl,* I thought—I would have. But a person with quadriplegia is at the mercy of a schedule. Bedtimes are strict. I can't hop out of bed if I hear a ding from a text message. I can't check my email at all hours of the night. I have to be put to bed by an attentive, hourly wage–earning caregiver, who has a life too. My scheduled bedtime routine started around nine thirty for most of the work week.

Plus, I wasn't ready to admit to the world that I was talking online quite regularly with a guy I hadn't even met yet. I didn't want to face the quizzical looks or skeptical comments from a caregiver who, because she had my back, would likely question a man who had hooked up with a quadriplegic over a personal computer. What kind of guy does this?

An amazing guy does this—one who likely rattled off a page or more of charming, inquisitive, compassionate discourse to me—and I was about to miss my window for a private reading!

If Rachel beats me to the house . . . rats, there she is!

Glancing into my rearview mirror, I saw her turning down my road. She'd been following me for who knows how long!

Come on, garage door, open. I'm in a hurry. When I think about it now, I can't believe the race I was in to enter the house before Rachel. *If I can just read his first paragraph . . .* I knew that would sustain me until I had more private time at my computer monitor—after Rachel's visit.

She entered just as I was squealing with excitement over the first few lines of Doug's reply. I felt her behind me as she looked over my shoulder at the screen and asked, "What is going on in here? I heard you scream from the garage. What's your good news now?"

Rachel had visited frequently the year before I met Doug Michaels. She knew I was busy with speaking engagements, edits to my first book, and prep for the Ms. Wheelchair USA contest. Likely, she would jump to some career-related conclusion regarding this outburst, since I had been nicknamed the Gingerbread Man long ago for my aversion to commitment. "You can't catch me," seemed to be my motto for years—especially after my last relationship had ended in so much personal pain that I had adopted a new mantra from a quote I found online: "Being single is not weak; it's being strong enough to wait for the right one." She would never guess this email was from a guy.

But I was bursting to tell someone about Doug, and Rachel was the perfect loyal friend with whom to share this secret.

"Okay, you can't tell anyone."

"Why not? If it's good news, why keep it a secret?"

"I'm seeing someone."

No words—just mouth wide open with an animated expression that said, "*You need to tell me more, girlfriend.*"

"Well, not really seeing. We haven't met in person yet."

Rachel's words still did not attach themselves to any sound, but I could almost read her lips: "Wow," or maybe "What?"

"We're both really busy, and he lives in Eau Claire . . . he works nights, so we're just getting to know each other . . . online."

I sensed a slight facial expression change from Rachel. *Online? Eau Claire?*

"Yep." I was reading her mind at this point. Her husband Jason grew up in the Eau Claire area. He knew everyone. If I told her that Doug was Doug Michaels from WQOW, chief meteorologist, Channel 18, Eau Claire TV, she would no doubt place Jason on a mission to prove that Doug was the decent man viewers saw and trusted on their nightly news.

Long pause. Mouth agape once again.

"I know it sounds a little scary—but you have to believe me, he's really special. Really different."

I wanted to say, "He's not a serial killer!" But that was my fear, already confronted with my sister Angie on the phone a few days before. She was the only other person I had confided in about my secret online man.

Angie: "Hey, Tasha. What's up?"

Me: "Is your computer handy? Can you check out something on the Internet?"

Angie: "Sure. What?"

Me: "Go to WQOW.com and click on the weather tab."

Angie: "Okay, but why?"

Me: "Click on the video where the guy is giving tonight's forecast."

Angie: "Yeah . . . so what?"

Me: "Does he look like a serial killer to you?"

I was doing my best to deflect any serial-killer fear Rachel might have. "That's awesome, Tasha! I'm so happy for you." Rachel was hugging and laughing with me now. "But how did all of this start? You didn't meet on—"

"ChristianMingle."

Long pause again.

"ChristianMingle? Seriously?"

"I know! I can't believe it either!"

Now we were both squealing and giggling like high school girls discussing the perfect prom date. Rachel knew that over the course of the past few months I had given into pressure—love life advice from various friends who encouraged me to "expand my horizons." That's code for "You must try everything, including online dating, if you think you're going to date in this complicated world." Rachel wasn't shocked that I was sifting through ChristianMingle—but she was puzzled that I found someone who was "date-worthy."

"It just seems like a bigger jungle out there when you look at it through the maze of dating websites." Rachel had met Jason at a wedding, and she thought the online process looked cluttered and scary.

"I know it sounds crazy," I admitted. "But I think I'm ready for more than online chatting with this guy. We're talking about meeting for coffee."

She eyed her watch. "Okay, Tasha, I have one hour to give you a good massage. You had better do some talking while I work on you. This I've gotta hear."

I had opened the can of worms. I had started an online dating connection, and it was out—at least to Angie and one trusted friend, Rachel. Her curiosity about a guy who at most was an electronic pen pal could not be ignored.

As soon as I opened Doug's profile, Rachel realized she didn't know him.

"But I'm gonna check with Jason. He knows everybody. And if he doesn't know this guy, he'll find out." Rachel and her husband Jason had a huge circle of friends and business contacts in western Wisconsin. No doubt someone would recognize Doug from TV.

Rachel is a gifted friend who will celebrate with me while simultaneously planning her strategy to get the goods on anyone who might threaten my safety and happiness. I would do the same for her if our situations were reversed. Who from a small-town, old-fashioned-values background *wouldn't* question an online romance with a complete stranger—especially for a friend with a disability? In fact, I was the biggest skeptic of them all. Consider my college friend Forrest, who has used a wheelchair since childhood because he was born with spina bifida. When he started an online relationship, I challenged him about the motives of the woman he began talking with rather regularly.

"Forrest, seriously. She's from Canada? Don't you think she's just trying to work her way into the country? This seems very fishy to me."

By the way, he has been happily married to this wonderful woman for many years.

Online dating was not even a last resort for me. I refused to consider it a viable option for meeting a man. That is, until my good friend Vernessa propelled me into trying ChristianMingle.

Up until then, I was chronically single. If you read my first book, you know how resistant I was to dating and how absorbed I was in my studies and my business success soon after.

Career was my focus. My initial five hundred flyers and pamphlets promoting me as a professional public speaker had prompted a steady demand for appearances for a variety of topics and audiences. Although seemingly random, my approach was working, and I was learning from some rather eclectic opportunities at schools, churches, health-care settings, and—believe it or not—prisons. My dream was becoming reality; my college majors of communication studies, music, and theology were serving me well. And the best part, I was passionate in my professional pursuits. I wanted more. I thrived on busy. And as long as I was healthy and had a reliable roster of caregivers in my corner to keep this professional pace going, I was on a literal and figurative roll.

My independence had led me to design and supervise the construction of my own home. With the support of family and friends, I moved out of Mom's house—the one that had been carefully designed for me during my interim stays at the Rochester Ronald McDonald Rehabilitation House and the Carr family home in Ellsworth. In fact, Al Hines, the same talented builder who had made my first handicap-accessible home—where Mom remains today after my parents split in 2004—also built my new dream house.

From my home-based office, I worked to finalize my first book, *My Last Step Backward*. I applied and received word that Ms. Wheelchair USA was within reach, and I said yes to almost every professional speaking request I received that first year in my new home. Upgrades on my van, plus a few electronic features in my house, facilitated my independence. I fully expected to grow my speaking circuit and fill my calendar to capacity. Yet, despite my surging confidence and all of my professional success, something was still missing.

I knew it was the sting from my last relationship. This bad breakup combined with the inevitable question at almost every school presentation—"Do you have a boyfriend?"—made me feel a void when asked about my personal happiness.

WITH MY THIRTIETH BIRTHDAY on the horizon, this void came racing to my attention. It couldn't be ignored. God wanted me to get married. I was sure of it.

"I'm single now, but I definitely plan on getting married and having children in the future," was my usual answer to curious audience members. I tried my best to cover. I had almost convinced myself that I didn't want a man in my current life. I leaned on my mantra, which implied I would wait patiently for Mr. Right, no matter how long it took. But, after my last relationship, everything changed. I didn't miss that man—he was abusive and manipulative, and I would never go back to that again—but I missed being part of a couple. Through him, I had discovered the joys of couplehood, and I wanted that again—the way it was in the beginning of the relationship, before he showed his true colors.

Unfortunately, I knew I was filling my days with so much stuff, so much busyness, that Mr. Right couldn't find me if he tried. It was as if I had a perpetual message, like one of those automatic email replies programmed for a vacation: "Sorry, I'm out of the office and not available for anything fun or personal . . . especially if you are male. But I'll get back to you as soon as I return from my professionally overscheduled lifestyle." Who would wait for me to be available after hearing this message? Your guess was as good as mine.

A familiar feeling returned. A cloud of insecurity regarding the most intimate self-doubts. The what-ifs had reared their ugly heads again. In the midst of all this professional growth and clamor, I had a constant, silent voice going off in my mind: What if I had waited too long? What if I had ignored too many interested guys who had asked me out throughout college? What if Ryan, one of my closest college friends, one of the best human beings I knew in the world, now happily married, could have been the one? If only I had reciprocated when he wanted to take our friendship to the next level.

At that time, during and shortly after college, I considered single status a step in my maturity. The Old Tasha always had a boyfriend. I had needed to have a man in my life, and that need to belong to someone became a sign of insecurity in my eyes. Perhaps a different type of uncertainty was starting—one where I did not feel worthy of a man's interest. Maybe this was all a fear of rejection, which led to my commitment to solitude. Who knows? But these were stages in my growing up that made me question later why I hadn't been more decisive when it came to securing a lifelong relationship.

"I'm just not ready. I'm too busy working on me. I have to focus on the inner me. There's no time for dating." Out loud to Angie, or to Mom, I could press a playback button in my head twenty-four seven. I had brain-washed myself into waiting. How could I be part of a couple when I had so much pain to work through—the pain of rejection from my boyfriend in high school, the pain of living with a disability with such a loss of my independence, the pain of my parents' divorce? There were also painful childhood memories from times when others took advantage of me.

Just as the playback button was pushed again, another one seemed synchronized with the worst what if of them all: What if God is playing a cruel trick on me?

What if He had tried to get my attention with the best match of them all and I was too self-absorbed to even notice? Had I been so caught up in my own personal success that I missed God's plan? Was He punishing me for ignoring the signs? Would I now have to deal with being single forever?

In retrospect, I know how ridiculous it sounds to imagine God would punish me or play a trick, when all He has ever been is supportive, encouraging, and reassuring. But that's where my fears took me not long after my breakup.

My mind would drift back to the days of rehab—long, lonesome hours lost in my thoughts of paralysis, imprisoned in a body that hadn't yet learned a new set of mobility rules. My greatest fears would smother my hopes for future joys like marriage and children. With the most trusted staff of nurses and therapists who pressed me to "ask anything," I sometimes opened up to the big topics. More than once, I had been told, "Yes, Tasha, you can get married—and even have children!"

Were they wrong? Would I spend the rest of my life as a single woman? Not because of physical limitations from my fall, but because I missed my chance by ignoring Mr. Right. Maybe I was too self-consumed for too many years with adapting to the New Tasha Schuh's lifestyle. Or maybe the time had come to face the truth: I feared rejection.

I fought my thoughts and relied on God to take me forward, but in the deepest recesses of my brain, I pondered a rather dark question for a strong Christian: *Has God abandoned me to a life alone, with no partner to love me, just when I feel I have all this love to give?*

Faith is a funny thing. When you think yours is strong enough to inspire others, one of life's greatest challenges will take you by surprise. Stuffing it was no longer my solution. I had grown in the sense that I could admit to family and friends that I was struggling. But how should I move forward? Little did I know that this uncertainty would bring a new and most important chapter to my life.

Turning thirty that year was magnifying my marital status situation. I obsessed over thoughts of it. *I waited too long. Everyone is married; why did I do this? Why did I wait? Everywhere I go, I hear, "Who are you dating? Who is your boyfriend?" I can't get away from it. It's almost comical!* I recall hosting a New Year's Eve party for twenty people—or was it nineteen, because I think everyone had a date except me. I took inventory and sure enough, I was the only single person at my own party.

A dear friend from church, Vernessa, shared my predicament. In her late thirties, she had moved back to Wisconsin after some years in Florida. We began hanging out together because, frankly, we were about the only single women in our church! Vernessa had confided in me that she truly wanted to be married and had been interested in finding the "right one" since she was about twenty years old. I thought, *Wow, and I've only been at this for a few months! I can't imagine wishing, and hoping, and looking for the right guy for years!*

Whether she knew it or not, Vernessa was showing me Who was in control. God's definition of patience was clearly different than mine. It didn't matter what I wanted or when I thought a man would fit conveniently into my life. I had to trust God's plan. I had to relax and know that He would provide the best way of life for me. This was going to be harder than I thought!

After my breakup with the guy I will simply refer to as the Bad Boyfriend, I found plenty of time to hang out with Vernessa.

That is, until she met Mr. Right—which didn't seem to take long at all.

One evening at dinner, she confided, "I'm trying an online service: ChristianMingle." Sure enough, three days into it—only three days of searching, scrutinizing, and filtering for the potential man of her dreams— she met the special guy she would eventually marry. And all I kept thinking was, *I will never try something like that.*

I have to hand it to Vernessa; it took months to wear me down. While she was dating her future husband, I was fighting her pleas. She would say, "Come on, Tasha, just try this. Just sign up. What have you got to lose? You never even have to contact someone. Just shop around a little, and see if it's for you."

"No, no, no! This will never happen, Vernessa."

I strongly objected every time Vernessa meandered to this topic. I admit, I had some pretty narrow, preconceived ideas about shopping for a date on a computer, and I vowed I would never, ever do it. It's ironic, I know. For a person who devotes her life to dispelling myths—to spreading the truth about the joy of life from a wheelchair and the fulfillment that can be found when mobility is lost—many myths of online dating festered in my mind. I chose to live in my ignorance and operate by these "truths":

1. Only desperate men use an online service (and we all know what they are desperate for . . .)

2. Creeps will fool you with lies and fake photos (big incomes, six-pack abs, full heads of hair . . .)

3. Even if a good guy like Vernessa's is spotted, who'd seriously want to date a woman with quadriplegia? (I post my picture, sitting in my chair; and no one replies . . .)

And my favorite dramatic scenario of all:

4. This is where women meet serial killers!

Clearly, it would take an act of God to get me to dispel my own personal myths about the proper way to meet men. Small-town Wisconsin girls found their future spouses in the most wholesome settings: college, church events, work, and bars.

It was true; when I took inventory of my closest married friends and family and how they hooked up romantically, many had met their significant others at social events that took place in establishments I didn't care to frequent. And the fact that sobriety was my healthy lifestyle choice due to the medications I needed and the mistakes I had made in college, I was not likely to meet my future husband in a nightclub or bar.

Despite all of the reasons I would in all likelihood not meet Mr. Right in one of the usual places, I stuck by my rationale that if God wanted me to get married, He would put someone in my path.

Unfortunately, that path had been free and clear for about a year's time. And Vernessa knew it.

Although busy with the new love of her life, Vernessa and I continued to hang out on a regular basis. Her happiness was contagious, but I was adamant each week, saying, "No way! I am not signing up! I will not create a login, I will not present a personal profile. Stop asking me!"

Finally, at the end of dinner one evening, Vernessa, seemingly out of angles and ploys, stated, "Fine. I'll do it for you."

"What?! No you won't."

"I can. I know enough about you to answer the profile questions. And you know I have pictures. I'll crop a good one. You know I have lots from hanging out together. So, there. Consider it done." Vernessa was not joking. She was having fun with me, but I could tell she meant business.

Annoyed but finally ready to prove that I was right all along, that no one would be interested in meeting a woman with quadriplegia online, I said, "Alright, but let me do it. How long's the minimum subscription? Didn't you say it's free for a trial period? I really do not want to pay for this." I gave her a look that said, *I'm caving in, my friend, but let me do this my way.*

Vernessa smiled with hopeful cheers. "Good!" she said. "There's no free trial, but fees don't kick in until you reach out to start a conversation with someone. You are going to be pleasantly surprised! Get ready for your next date!"

My last date had been months ago—but it felt like years. And even after creating a profile with a three-month subscription, I didn't intend to get too caught up or hopeful about the whole thing. (Ironically, I was starting my profile on September 19, which meant this account would expire on my thirty-first birthday.) Once I clicked "submit," I just assumed my homework was done, and I could report back to Vernessa with, "See, I told you so. Not one email from an entire network of Christian men."

But September 20, just one day after subscribing, the messages started.

"What is going on?" I said to myself as my inbox seemed to be backed up with unexpected contacts. I had logged into my email as usual, expecting questions regarding my next speaking commitment.

I scrolled and scrolled and finally realized what was happening. My email was full of notifications. I had to then navigate to the ChristianMingle website, click on their profiles, and figure out who these guys were. But by the time I toggled back to the message page—remember, my motor skills are very limited—there was a whole new slew of them!

Who has time for this?!

Well, I began making time. I admit, I was curious. I recall connecting with one guy. We had a nice introductory online chat. But when he wrote, "So, when can we talk again? This time tomorrow is good for me . . ." I found myself scrolling through my calendar and replying, "Uh, not tomorrow, sorry . . . maybe Wednesday . . . oh, sorry, I'm gone then, too. Looks like I'm free . . . in a week?"

Not exactly the captivating closure expected from a potential date.

Vernessa did a good job of convincing me that I should make myself more available. "But you need to get organized," Vernessa reminded me. This site required management, like any online system. "Or the good ones will get lost in the crowd!"

Well, I am paying the monthly Mingle fees . . . I mean, if I'm in, I'm all in. Which meant I would give it a valiant effort to at least say I tried it. Then I could tell Vernessa and others that it didn't work for me.

This was about the time I sought a new employee for hire. Not another caregiver, but a life coach. I had spoken at a women's networking event where I met Michelle. Her professional title intrigued me.

Life coach . . . what is that? I could infer somewhat from her role at the event, but didn't think much more about it.

One night, after a full day of meetings, life felt so chaotic. I saw an email from Michelle. I clicked, and sure enough, the perfect phrase appeared on my screen: "From Chaos to Clarity." It was Saturday night at a quarter to ten, and I picked up the phone to leave a message with the woman who had coined the most meaningful motto—music to my ears.

I got her voicemail. She quickly returned my call the next day. It seemed meant to be.

I realized immediately that Michelle was not only gifted at her job of organizing busy professional people, but she also won her clients' trust. She possessed an acute ability to see a lack of balance in a busy life. All work and no play brought Tasha considerable anxiety, which I needed to acknowledge if I truly expected to change the pattern.

Through our conversations, a key word popped up for Michelle: organization. More explicitly, I needed to downsize.

"Tasha, I think God has more in His plan for you. But God can't make a move until you make some room."

After numerous conversations and close analysis of my calendar, perhaps the most unexpected lesson I was learning from Michelle was to say no.

"Let's look at this week for example. You have speaking commitments, right? Most of them involve travel time, which doubles your clock hours for the job. You may or may not be getting compensation for this."

Michelle made a good point. I often broke even or lost money on agreements I made. But I figured this was common for most people starting a small business. I just hoped that some of the more lucrative events helped balance things out.

As my life coach, she understood this business theory and agreed. Yet she continued to point out the big picture.

"You have volunteer duties on the side. I know you are committed to this. And freelancing hours as a speaker often forces you to change your schedule. Fortunately, most of these things are flexible. But this is perhaps adding to the stress. You still worry about coming through for everyone. So you end up working weekends, which should be free for a social life.

"Then there are those times when you get the call to action. A tragedy occurs . . . a victim of an accident knows your story, or the medical staff and family involved do. You visit people at Courage Center, Rochester Mayo, an area hospital, or someone's home as soon as a contact is made. Even if it is only a phone contact, that time must be accounted for and calculated into your busy day." Michelle's interview questions had led her to a spot-on analysis of where my time was going.

"But this is what I do. This is why I am speaking; so I can make people aware and hopefully help in some way. To give hope and to motivate them to carry on. To prove that it'll get better."

"I understand that, Tasha. This is what makes you tick and what drives you to manage a busy life. Plus, it's incredibly admirable. Everyone should follow your model. We'd all be a lot happier if our goal was to improve life for others. But you must recognize the time and expense involved with this level of altruism. We have to factor it in."

"Well, my goal is to be speaking full time. But I don't even have time to follow up on inquiries or get the information when event planners try to contact me. All these other things are keeping me from doing what I know I am called to do—what I've known since my junior year at Winona State."

Fortunately, Michelle supported my speaking goals. But she continued with a laundry list of other responsibilities which I had taken on, gratis and without any proof that my time and expenses could or would be compensated. For instance, I served on four boards—all organizations supporting people with disabilities.

"Tasha, sometimes you are volunteering so much that there is not time to speak when an invitation comes along. You are on the road to burnout if you don't reclaim some of your hours. Then who will you be helping?"

Her evidence was building, but the most poignant item on her list was when she said, "And no man's going to fit into this schedule."

I suddenly felt like I was stuffing it again—like I was covering a missing link when I told audiences I was truly happy. Was I faking it? I knew in my heart I was not.

My life is better because of my accident. I say this in my presentations, and I mean it! Yet it was time to admit that all work and no play made Tasha a bit of a hypocrite.

I had a revelation at this point: *Tasha, if your speeches promote the belief that happiness can be found wherever you are, you have to practice what you preach. You have to find balance. You have to pay attention to God's plan.*

That's when Michelle and I began to talk openly about my love life—or lack thereof. She asked, "So, how's your love life?"

I had to be honest. "What love life?" I think I used the word "nonexistent."

"Hmmm . . . that's funny."

"Funny?" I replied.

"Well, I just have a feeling that this will be changing soon. He's right around the corner."

"What? Who?" Then I admitted that I was dabbling with ChristianMingle.

"See! Things are about to change for you! And the next time we meet, I want to hear that you went on a date."

I do think Michelle had a bit of a premonition that day. On our third date or so, Doug and I were at Caribou Coffee, and in walked Michelle.

But I'm getting ahead of myself. Like I said, I had my work cut out for me!

CHAPTER TWO

IT STARTS WITH A SMILE

I N NOVEMBER, MY FRIEND Melissa visited. During our college days at Winona State University, Melissa and I pledged to dodge any serious romance. School and friendship were far more important. Ha! That pledge didn't last. At this point, Melissa was married and living in a Chicago suburb, already the mother of the first of her children. I was happy for her when she got married, since this occurred in that stage of my life where I had no interest in my own marital status. Marriage was some vague chapter I postponed for later.

Of course, the Bad Boyfriend changed everything.

Before him, I can recall many times I turned down dates or accepted a casual dating offer with reluctance. Those unexpected encounters with men who pursued me frequently led to a one-date experience. No one could say I didn't try! My mom, and sometimes Angie, pushed me to consider casual dating. Right after college, I caved in and accepted a few offers, thinking that, although dating scared me, it was part of my future. Maybe I needed "practice."

I met a guy at a Casting Crowns concert—Josiah. He walked up to me and said, "I love your hair." How many guys pay attention to that? I was impressed. And he truly overlooked my disability as we easily started talking. I learned that, many months earlier, he had completed the Minnesota Teen Challenge program for drug and alcohol rehabilitation. Through mutual friends, I found out that he had stated, "God is telling me, Tasha is the one I'm going to marry."

I was flattered. Yet my first reaction was, "I'm not interested in dating now." In so many words, I told Josiah this on the phone. Grateful for the offer, I felt I'd dodged another person trying to accelerate my plan. But when Angie heard I had turned him down, she persuaded me to reconsider.

"What can one date hurt! Just go out and have fun."

"But he told people he wants to marry me. That's a little much, don't you think?" I replied.

"That's just talk," she rebutted "Go out, and find out if he's even a nice guy. You make your mind up before you even give someone a chance."

"Okay—but I'm not leading him on. I'm just gonna be me." No romantic designs. No chance that he'll be attracted to me. I wore brown sweatpants when we met for coffee at Starbucks.

Angie was right. He was a nice guy, a special person whose passion was with God. I was impressed and excited for his future, but Josiah needed a partner who was ready for commitment. I had goals of my own. He moved away, and I'm sure he is helping others through life.

Another near miss occurred when I had a flat tire on my way to an appointment in Rochester. I had OnStar in my Pontiac van, and the service guy they sent me was really friendly.

"You're really cute. Here's my number—call me. I'd like to take you out on a date sometime."

"Okay," I replied. "Thanks for all of your help."

I will never call him.

But God said, *Call him. Get out of your comfort zone.* I debated with God for days, and then I couldn't believe it; I actually picked up the phone. This served as practice, all right, although I was a nervous wreck!

We met at a Caribou Coffee in Rochester, and we did have a nice time discovering we both went to Winona State. But I learned he was quite a bit older than me and our college years were far apart. I could tell we had very different interests. We talked a couple more times over the phone, but then I stopped returning his calls.

God, I know You think this is a good thing, but I can't see it. I know You think I should get married, but I'm not feeling it. I'll marry sometime . . . when I'm fifty-five. But not now. If You really want me to start looking for the right match, something's gotta change. What are You going to do to make me want to get married?

That was my prayer. I talked with God about this so often, especially after I met someone who showed interest. What was the change that would have to occur for me to want, welcome, and reciprocate these romantic feelings for someone?

One date here, another date there. This series of casual social outings never led to a relationship—until I fell hard for someone. Unfortunately, he turned out to be the opposite of Mr. Right. Despite the pain this induced, however, I have no regrets today. Who could have predicted so many lessons rolled into one boyfriend?

My pattern of casual dates ended when I was reintroduced to a guy from my childhood. He had always lived in a neighboring town. After not seeing him for years, I unexpectedly met him at a church event. It hit me much later that this was only three weeks after I started asking God for motivation to marry.

This guy, too, pushed for a serious relationship, and this time I fell. Hard. We began dating in March. We had broken up by July. In retrospect, that sounds so short. But it was fast and intense. I fell in love with his sweetness. I fell for the joy of his companionship, his warm embrace, his attentiveness. But when it turned—when he lost the facade of "having it all together"—I learned the hard way that I had not really fallen for him, but for couplehood.

This is why all my friends want a boyfriend! This is why every girlfriend I know wants to be married! And this is why some fall hard for the wrong guy.

After our breakup, I suffered from the loss of my new identity—a woman with a significant other in her life. But, as it took me months to realize, I needed to stay strong for the right one. He was out there. And for the first time in my life, I wanted to find him.

Occasionally, I talked about this relationship in my speaking events, and it's covered somewhat in my first book. But now, years later, reflecting back on this guy I thought would be the one, I have new perspective. I can't ignore the point where he turned on me, where his love and attention took a one-eighty, where he lost his temper and his ability to see my gifts.

To his credit, the Bad Boyfriend had experienced a transformation sometime before we started dating. Five years prior, he had joined AA and quit a pattern of partying he had embraced when I first met him as a teenager. In fact, that's why our paths crossed to begin with—we had mutual drinking friends. I, however, had moved on to college, dropped my own partying ways, and thought I would never see him again. When he showed up at a church event, sober and proud of his self-improvement, I was intrigued. I discovered that, during the two years leading up to this, he had devoted much time to his growing faith.

I was still in my chronically single stage of life after college. People would tell me, "He wants to date you, Tasha. Spend some time with him."

"Nope—not interested," was my reaction. Unfortunately, there's a link to alcohol abuse on my dad's side of the family. I had no interest in being in a relationship with someone who had the possibility of falling back into this.

But he was relentless. He began to show up regularly at my church on Sundays. He offered to cook for me. He persisted, and finally, I agreed to "hang out" with him, thinking, *This is not dating.*

But one thing led to another, and we were a couple.

He was so sweet . . . for a while. Yet this faded quickly. And just about the time I had fallen in love with the idea of having a relationship, his anger and impatience showed their true colors.

He convinced me that he was the only one who was honest with me.

"No one tells you the truth, Tasha. They can't. You're paralyzed. You're a local celebrity. Do you think anyone is going to be honest to your face? I'm the only one who will tell you the truth."

Gradually, I believed him. This was the start of his stranglehold on me— his power to tell me I was stupid, and naive, and nothing without him.

It started small, with my GPS. His job required all kinds of driving in the Twin Cities. He knew his way everywhere. But when I drove in St. Paul, Minneapolis, or any metro suburb, my habit was to set my navigator.

"I can't believe you need that thing. How long have you been driving in the Cities? Stupid people rely on those things. Anyone with a brain can find their way around this metro area."

Other times when we argued about the silliest things, like my Bluetooth, he would blow up. When I challenged him on his quick judgment, his anger escalated. When he pounded his fist on my kitchen table out of frustration, he claimed that it was my fault.

"I don't have anger issues. You push me to this. If you'd think before you said something, we'd get along just fine."

When I suggested that he had issues that made him fly off the handle too quickly, he said, "I dealt with all of that. I finished my twelve-step program. I don't drink anymore, because I worked it all out. You are the one who has issues."

Clearly, this guy was not the one. Yet I was so brainwashed, so manipulated into believing his criticisms of me, that I was trying to "fix" me. I believed him when he said that I triggered a negative response in him. I felt guilty and tried so hard to just get along with him. In the process, I lost my voice. I began to believe that I was the source of any disagreements we had. So many repressed thoughts haunted me, and I took full responsibility for them. So much so that he broke up with me. And I was left obsessing over how to win him back.

Too many relationships go wrong early on, and people miss the warning signs. I want to help women be strong enough to resist this. I want to help men to be better than this! I am saddened by stories of women who endure this—or worse. I recall a woman who confided in me soon after this guy broke it off.

"I just left my husband . . . I can't believe it. Me, alone with our kids. But I'm sick of hiding under the kitchen table in our own home. I'm tired of the bruises and the black eyes."

I knew at that moment, if I had stayed in that relationship, it would have gone this way. I kept it from my family—covered for him—until it was completely over. My parents, Angie, and my friends Brooke and Holly were all shocked, appalled, and so relieved I came to my senses.

I share this stuff now, not to bash one guy who clearly has some work to do, but for all the readers who can learn from my short but painful experience, my near-disaster. I share this for all the women who feel trapped, with or without kids, who need to find the courage to make a move. I share this to warn others: Don't believe it when an abuser says, "You'll never find anyone else. No one will put up with you. You'll never be able to make it alone."

Our relationship was short, but it was a major loss for me. I felt like someone died when he broke it off. Yet the hurt caused by this breakup probably fueled my healing. My sadness over losing him soon turned to anger. He hurt me. The fact that he didn't have it in him to work on himself in order to stay in my life was so frustrating. With time I saw that it was a blessing in disguise. It took a while, but I have forgiven him, and I now pray for him. Looking back, I can finally appreciate the fact that he came into my life when God said, *Tasha, you still have more to learn.*

The lessons were many! I needed to learn to discern between a man who loved me and a man who needed power over someone. I needed to learn to trust that a man could change my life for the better. It's ironic that a bad relationship set me on the path to a better one. I will always be indebted to this experience for helping me see the joys of companionship and for teaching me what to avoid in a man.

The lessons I learned perhaps made me cautious, but they left me craving more. Discovering how much I enjoyed being with someone, like in the beginning stages of our dating, made me want to persevere. I had done so much alone for so many years that I had forgotten what this kind of companionship felt like. And I liked it! Many years later, I am over the resentment and actually grateful that he turned out to be wrong for me. It meant I was available to meet Doug! And, because of the independence I gained due to his criticisms, I was far more prepared to make my relationship with Doug a success.

I'm sure it was an "I'll show him" attitude, but our breakup drove me to want to learn the things in which he found fault. For instance, I was criticized for depending upon a caregiver to come in every evening around dinner time. Because of this frustration, I set out to learn how to insert my own catheter, at home or when on the road. (A year after my accident,

I had my bladder rerouted to my bellybutton, yet still had caregivers performing the procedure at the time we were dating.) His observations, followed by negative commentary, made me want to get my own plate from fridge to microwave, without a caregiver's help. When he saw a caregiver pour pills into my mouth, his reaction made me self-conscious enough to do something about it. Soon, I learned to administer my own medication. These are only a few things; believe me, he nitpicked about everything. These legitimate cares that I could complete on my own were spurred on by his caustic remarks. Once I learned how to do these things, I no longer needed someone to do them for me. Funny how we are often motivated by the negative.

Had I not been in this relationship, I would have had trouble meeting Doug in another town. Our dates likely would have taken place in Ellsworth only. More independence meant I was ready for the relationship of a lifetime. In the end it proved to be practice—just what I needed.

"TASHA, LOOK AT THE load of messages you have!" Melissa brought me back to ChristianMingle. She gazed over my shoulder at the mess of emails I had essentially ignored, and she immediately took Vernessa's side in the issue. "Don't delete them, Tasha. You just need a system."

So many men had initiated contact with me by sending a canned one-liner or a "smile." Row after row of lines ranging from, "Hi, I just wanted to send you a smile," from the website's 'Casual' category, to phrases from the 'Flirty' category like, "I'm not very good at flirting, but can I practice with you?" This might have been fun flattery from the right guy. But when it came from a man as old as my father, it seemed a little creepy.

"Yikes, Melissa, delete that! I'm not interested in dating my dad's friends!" This was just a figure of speech, since I never really knew any of the men, age-appropriate or otherwise, who "smiled" at me. The bottom line: all of this was a fun game to play with friends, but deep down, it made me even more cautious about an online service.

Melissa and I laughed and spent the better part of her weeklong visit organizing my Mingle Mail messages and smiles. If nothing else, it became an avenue for us to talk and share some girlfriend time on a subject that I had been stuffing. Thinking about it all alone in my own head brought me nothing but more worry and self-doubt. Acting on it, even in a playful way, made it seem like a game.

But sure enough, after Melissa spent hours placing all my contacts into "Yes," "Maybe," and "No" folders and left my house for Illinois, I jumped right back into my pattern of work. I completely forgot about Melissa's folders. I started to feel overwhelmed again by receiving so many messages. Until the night of my birthday, the night I put all of this back in God's hands.

December 19, 1980: I was the final Schuh baby—the third child for Duane and Kathy—who came home from the hospital packed in a holiday stocking. On this particular birthday, thirty-one years later, I said goodnight to the friends who had gathered at my home for cake and conversation, and then I rolled over to my computer to check my emails. Filtering through birthday wishes and work-related messages, I considered the fact that my ChristianMingle subscription was expiring that night after midnight.

Yes, my account would expire exactly three months after I signed up. September 19 through December 19. *I am done being attentive to this.* I hadn't realized it at sign-up time, but now as the three-month mark was on the horizon, it seemed very noticeable and kind of ironic. After all of the reflection this three-month experience provided—and essentially forced me into—cutting it off on my thirty-first birthday provided perfect timing. A sort of present to myself.

Okay, this is it! I've tried hard enough. God is not playing a trick on me. I am going about it all wrong. The fact that I am making this effort—that I am trying to manipulate my life to find a man—says that something is wrong with this picture.

With God's help, I manage my life just fine!

It's true, I cherish this gift of a second chance after my accident.

I need to show gratitude for it. I just had a wonderful evening with friends who love me. I'm a different Tasha—a stronger, wiser Tasha. I need to quit looking for a man, like I'm shopping from a catalog, to make me complete.

Regardless of the busy thoughts my birthday and Mingle Mail had stirred up, my scheduled bedtime once again ended my day. I had learned to keep a mental journal at night—a gratitude list in my mind. So, the night of my birthday, I took virtual inventory of all the joys in my full life—all the blessings that proved that nothing was absent since God provided all I needed or wanted. The only thing to add was an attitude adjustment, to acknowledge how blessed I was at age thirty-one.

What could possibly be missing? Not one thing. Constant companionship? Do I need a man by my side to fight off loneliness?

Actually, there is little alone time for a person with quadriplegia, if you're as active as I've chosen to be. My cares dictate plenty of social interaction if I intend to get out of bed early each day, prepare for a variety of tasks and van rides, and get back in bed at night for the necessary sleep to start the whole cycle over again.

With a growing career in public speaking, companionship was not my issue. Despite my first book's chapter "The Loneliness of Dependency," where I described the pain of being surrounded by people with no idea what I was enduring, so much had changed from this early stage of my condition.

Initially after my accident, I felt that empathy was not even possible. This definitely made me feel alone in the world. This was a normal early stage of paralysis. I was still healing and adapting to a changed life.

By age thirty-one, however, I had spent almost half of my life in a wheelchair. I had come so far in my independence. I had met plenty of people who dealt with similar circumstances. I was not alone. Even nondisabled friends, medical staff, and family proved they didn't need to roll in my chair to show compassion without pity.

So by now I had reached the point where I controlled much of my personal contact with others. I scheduled my caregivers, I communicated with career contacts, and I traveled to my speaking gigs. This kind of self-sovereignty had a way of eliminating loneliness, and I loved being in charge. Unless some fluke of fate, like a health setback—which I worked diligently to avoid—kept me from connecting with the world, I topped the charts for social interaction most days of my life.

My caregiver relationships have been some of the strongest connections of all. Even by the end of my first book, I was detailing my desire to keep family as just that—family. I gradually discharged all of my family caregivers, except my nieces, who were just coming of age and learning to work for me. With complete confidence that my biggest go-to team, Mom and Angie, was a phone call away and only a few miles from my house, I tried my best to leave the caregiver role to the professionals. And thus, the women I hired to assist me knew every aspect of my life. I rarely craved conversation since it occurred organically throughout my day.

So, what was missing? Maybe children? Was this my worry? That life would not feel complete without kids? My nieces and nephews were the amazing new loves of my life. Just because I hadn't given birth to them didn't mean that I loved them any less. I recall holding each and every one of them when they were infants and thinking, *I will be the best auntie on earth! I want to hold them as babies, entertain them at my house, have sleepovers, watch them grow up, and create a bond so strong that they'll feel like they have a third parent!*

Isabel, Anna, and Ella have always lived in the Ellsworth area, just a short drive from my home. Angie's three beautiful daughters have taken turns riding my wheelchair since they were old enough to climb onto my lap. My sister and her husband, so strong during my recovery, have been exceptional parents, managing a challenging work situation. Angie runs the home front, along with working a full-time job, while Scott makes two annual eight-week trips to the Ukraine to help in his father's agricultural business.

And then there are the boys—my handsome nephews Cameron and Connor. They have always lived away from Pierce County. I wanted to free up time for these out-of-towners, too. Ryan and Nikki, their hardworking parents, have always worked such full schedules. So it made more sense for me to drive to them every couple of months or so.

This mental monologue accompanied my special birthday gathering. I made a final decision that night: when all contacts disappeared with my expiring ChristianMingle account, I would let go of these messages forever. I saw this date coming and was relieved because I was tired of trying to communicate with so many new people. Online dating was not the answer for me. I would let this fade into cyberspace for good.

Suddenly, a summer memory seized my mind. I saw myself out on the deck reading Joni Eareckson Tada's book entitled *Choices, Changes*. This book has been uplifting on so many levels. Yet, at that moment, while questioning my single status in a world of couples, I recalled the profound sadness triggered while reading one episode in Joni's story—a fear that I might never kiss a man again.

Joni was always on my radar because she was one of the few public women who had a similar injury. Hers was a swimming accident, different than mine in how it happened but similar in her degree of paralysis. She's been one of the few females with quadriplegia—Darcy Pohland, my role model and friend from WCCO, was another—who shared her life publicly. But after Darcy passed away in 2010, I definitely felt a void in who I could look to for inspiration.

Joni's first book, *Joni: An Unforgettable Story*, written thirty years before my injury, eventually became a staple in my personal library. In fact, I owned multiple copies because so many people had given me this book as a gift upon my accident. I had watched her movie, but during those years when I dodged romance, Joni's personal struggles with love did not interest me. Her difficult search for a man who would accept her unconditionally was a struggle I had postponed. I just wasn't ready for that part of her experience. I was trying to accept myself unconditionally first; couplehood would have to come later. So I didn't really read Joni until that summer after my own painful relationship ended, and my deep desire to be loved started.

That summer—in the months after the bad breakup—my perspective changed. I picked up Joni's book, and as I read, an overpowering realization hit me: I might never, ever feel the returned love of a man again.

While reading, I had reached the part where Joni described playing herself in her own movie—a biographical film depicting her struggles finding love now that her accident had changed her life so dramatically. Joni described the odd juxtaposition of kissing an actor who played a guy she had once dated.

As the director yelled "action," Joni knew she had to relive a kiss, something she hadn't felt for over a decade. She had been so engrossed in her work, which included writing, speaking, and now making a movie—she'd forgotten this. It was as if she was feeling a man's lips on her own, in this case from a stranger, for the first time. Oddly, she heard the word "cut" and woke up to the reality that this was only a stage direction, a reenactment, a cinematic manifestation that aroused feelings not reciprocated by her scene partner.

That summer day, Joni's words spoke to me in a way her writing had never spoken to me before. I understood her. I felt her void. I wondered if I would ever feel a kiss on my lips from a man who wanted me and truly loved me.

The impact of her words, and the recent memory of a brief romantic relationship with someone I thought loved me in return, had me wanting another chance. I worried that I had missed my window and waited too long to find love.

I cried that afternoon as I read Joni's words. I knew exactly how she was feeling. And from that day forward, Joni Eareckson Tada became a force in my life. I would never again take for granted the depth of experience she shared. I would never again overlook the path she had paved for women who struggle with the unknowns that accompany paralysis.

Later, when I finally met Joni Eareckson Tada at a leadership conference in the Twin Cities where she spoke, I had the opportunity to tell her face-to-face how valuable her voice has been to someone like me. Meeting her in 2014 was a full-circle moment for me.

"HEY. HOW'S THE BIRTHDAY girl? Did you have a nice evening?" My caregivers entered my house the next morning to kick off another busy day.

By now, my Mingle Mail computer tab was gone. Yet only an hour's drive away, with a watchful eye on the weather, noting patterns that seemed to suggest a white Christmas for both of us, Doug Michaels clicked on my profile.

CHAPTER THREE

JUST ONE LAST LOOK

OUG HERE. INDEED, I did click on Tasha's picture. She was the most beautiful woman I had laid eyes on. Prior to this, entering the ninth page of my search, I was starting to wonder what I was doing; why was I spending so much time on ChristianMingle in the first place? Despite having a profession where I was in the public eye and often critiqued for my work, I was definitely more of an introvert. Give me a weather map and an audience, and I could shine. Approaching a woman to ask her out, even in my midthirties, made me nervous and uncomfortable. Having only a picture and brief personal profile to go on did not seem much different to me than asking out a complete stranger in a public setting. Cyberspace then became a much easier and less intimidating way of meeting someone. The simple fact that this worked out is only by the grace of God. When I sent that first smile, I didn't think I had a shot in the world at getting a response from TLovely99.

I certainly wasn't looking for a relationship on December 20, 2011, when I logged on to ChristianMingle just to search profiles. I had been living in Eau Claire, Wisconsin, for nine years at this point. You will gain some insight into my backstory—the path I took from growing up a shy kid in Detroit to the lead meteorologist for the ABC affiliate in Eau Claire— when you read my Mingle Mails to Tasha. Needless to say, however, the previous several months had featured an awakening of sorts in my life. In

April I had become a baptized follower of Jesus Christ, and since then my life was doing a complete one-eighty. While I had met some great people at my new church home, I was still not feeling like I was in a position to get serious with anyone. Church, along with work and spending time at the gym, were vying for 80 percent of my time. Deep down I had always had the desire to marry and possibly have children, but now at thirty-five, doubts began to creep in as to whether this would ever come to fruition. Resentments and disappointments from my past kept me guarded and, frankly, slow to admit that the desire to have a lifelong companion was still there.

I knew from talking with others that ChristianMingle was a way to meet someone who might have things in common with me—without spending a bunch of money on a monthly membership. I'd been scrolling through the website just enough to read some profiles and check out some pictures. But until I saw Tasha's photo, I had not once made a date with a woman registered with the site.

Of course, I had no idea that I had sent my smile the day after Tasha's birthday. A few days passed with no response, and I thought I could maybe chalk it up to the holidays.

It's December; people are busy with shopping, Christmas parties, baking . . . whatever. I'll give it a few days.

A full week went by . . . no reply.

Well, she's gorgeous. She's probably already met someone. She won't be back to the website—why would she?

New Year's evening I checked my ChristianMingle mail one last time. This time, I saw Tasha's response:

"Sure, let's talk. Can you tell me a little bit about yourself? - Tlovely99."

Wow, I felt myself sit up a little straighter in my chair. I read it again!

" . . . tell me a little bit about yourself." What should I say? How should I reply?

After waiting almost two weeks, certain that Tasha Schuh was engaged to someone else by now, she had smiled back at me.

I better think this through . . . but don't take too long. If she checks her Mingle Mail right away, I gotta have something there. I typed:

Hi,

First, I hope you had a great Christmas and New Year. Mine were very relaxing . . . with parents on Christmas, and on my couch for New Years! Well, I'm not sure where to begin but my name would probably be a good start! It's Doug. I live in Altoona and work as a meteorologist. The job is actually what brought me this way nine years ago. I was in Colorado for four years before this, going to school and absolutely loving the mountain view EVERY day. Growing up in Michigan, I'm used to these winters, but to be honest, as I get older I'm finding it harder to take the months of cold every winter. One nice thing about Colorado was the weather—pretty common to warm into the 40s and 50s at times during these months. Gosh, I'm sorry . . . was starting to get off on a weather tangent there. Guess since that's my job I can't help it! As for my faith . . . I grew up Lutheran. Went to a Lutheran grade and high school before heading off to U of Michigan for my first round of college. Loved it so much I had to go a second four years! I still consider myself a Lutheran, but I've learned over these past two years that being a Christ follower is much more about what's in the heart than in a title. I found this wonderful church here in Eau Claire two summers ago at a time when I was feeling alone and spiritually empty. I still feel I have things to accomplish in my journey with Christ but I'm back on the road and feeling very good about it. So that's a little about me. I'd love to tell you more, and I'd very much like to hear more about you. With that . . . have a great day/night and I look forward to hearing back from you!

I was pretty excited . . . but not overconfident. For one thing, Tasha had taken twelve days to respond to my initial smile, and then she took four or five days to reply to my "Hello, here's a bit about me" note. I knew enough about online correspondence not to get my hopes up. Sometimes these messages lead to a date, and sometimes you never hear back again. I waited and checked, waited and checked, and finally, Tasha reciprocated with more about her life.

And it was clear immediately that this was someone very special. Successful, happy, ambitious—and she wanted to know more about me.

I knew from her profile and her earliest note that her trust in God was firm and sincere. I was relieved that I could speak frankly—that she would understand the faith that was growing inside of me and my excitement over finding a good church family. Right away, conversation was easy with Tasha, which gave me hope that we would eventually meet. But I didn't want to be too pushy, either. Tasha had shared some details of her last speaking engagement—including an exchange between her and a girl in the audience, from which I could tell the girl was so moved and inspired. I was convinced this was a woman whose relationship with God had so much to teach me.

Here goes—note number two:

Happy Friday Tasha! I'm very glad to hear your travels went well and your speaking engagements were wonderful. It is truly touching—and rewarding—when you see someone respond like that girl did. That means you are reaching people, and through you, God is reaching them as well. Truly a gift that God has given to you! I must say that it's very cool you also sing—I do too, but my harmonies are probably not nearly as pleasant to the ears as yours. Nevertheless, I enjoy belting it out in church—(it helps that the person singing on stage has a microphone so it seems to enhance my abilities to blend in). It is rewarding to receive thank-yous from kids when I visit local schools, because I know that maybe some of them will look at science as fun instead of boring. As fun as talking to kids is, though, I just marvel at your ability to tell your story to people you don't even know and share how the Lord has used the accident to make you an even stronger, more positive person. It's definitely not easy telling people about things that are close to us sometimes, but when you think about it, that's what defines us as individuals. And we are all unique individuals—thankfully, because it would be awful if we were all the same! When I was in ninth grade, the first thing my religion teacher had us memorize was this: I am a unique child of God, full of potential! That was twenty-one years ago and I still remember it to this day.

To be honest, the paragraph that you wrote in your profile is what sealed the deal for me and ultimately led to the first 'smile'! I mean, pictures are nice, (and you are quite beautiful by the way), but it was your words that made me respond, (perhaps a little prodding from God too). I had received some smiles and correspondences from others, but when I logged onto here, your email was the one I was looking for!

Okay, I'll move on before I get too mushy. Oh, by the way, I love talking about Christ and my journey with him (and hearing about yours). That is something that was missing from many of my past dating experiences, but never again. If I become involved with someone, I want Christ to be in the center of that relationship. Eventually, I'll share more of my personal struggles with you and how I believe that God has used those to make me a better man. I know that he will show me the way as far as my future—I just need to be open and receptive to where it takes me. For so long I tried doing things my way without much long term success, so now I'm gonna start listening to what is put in my heart rather than what my brain wants me to do . . . God's time usually doesn't coincide with our time—(I know for a fact that my past prayers have been selfish and often self-centered with wanting things now), but you are most certainly right . . . he knows what's best for us in the long run.

Being an only child was kind of nice when I was growing up, but the older I get the more I wish that I had siblings. Everyone thinks only children are spoiled rotten, and to some degree I was spoiled as far as my parents could afford to spoil me. But they also taught me values and morals, and how to be a responsible, hardworking guy.

Funny story about my interest in the weather as a kid . . . I grew up in Detroit, Michigan, so as a kid my two favorite parts of the news were sports and weather. Eventually, weather jumped over sports! Anyway, I'd watch the weather, memorize the numbers and what our local TV guy talked about, then afterwards I would pretend I was the weatherman and do the weather show in my room, pretending to point at maps and talk about cold fronts, etc. Very nerdy, I know, but it started me on my way to my current profession!

I work for ABC in Eau Claire, which has various channel numbers depending on satellite, cable, antenna, etc. But . . . if you ever want to see a weather forecast from your friendly weatherman, you can go to www.WQPW.com and check out the weather video. The one I record is usually uploaded by 6pm.

For some reason, writing to Tasha was effortless. We connected through our mutual love of food and animals. We traded favorite musicians, finding so much overlap. We both loved songs of praise and faith and it was exciting to learn about new acts from Tasha as I was, admittedly, a few years behind.

I knew I had to stop and hit send, with hopes she would reply right away. But I also was beginning to get a grasp of her schedule. I won't pretend that I had any idea how long it took her to prep and send her messages back to me. But I was sensing that, disability or not, this was a woman who needed and deserved a patient man in her life. I started a habit of sending my emails promptly, yet I waited patiently for her replies.

Well, Miss Tasha, I must be off. It's payday, so that means grocery shopping and bill paying—how fun! A couple more totally random questions for you: have you ever ridden on a train before as part of your travels? And, since you like history . . . if you could pick one time period to travel back to and see firsthand, what would it be? I hope you have/had a great Friday, and I anxiously await your next email! —Doug

These long, friendly conversations progressed to the point where, after about three weeks, we finally exchanged phone numbers. Talking would be an easier form of communication for Tasha, and I looked forward to hearing her voice.

Many people have asked me, "When did you know it was time to ask Tasha out? Meet for a date?" I'm not sure; I was just trying to give it enough time. I think I sensed some hints from her when we talked on the phone at night, during my breaks between shows. She had given me her website and told me to visit it. In retrospect, I know she wanted me to be fully aware of her disabilities. But the website video at the time did not emphasize her limitations. It showed her getting into her van and sitting at her mom's house on the back deck. Well, it's Tasha! Of course, it's going to spotlight what she can do, not reveal what she cannot do. Her life is all about no limits, or at least adapting to them.

Anyway, I know we both felt it. It was getting closer to the right time to pop the question: *Will you date me?*

But wait—I had to let her know that I was going to put her first. Her concerns, her trepidations about dating, needed to be addressed. I didn't care that she was in a wheelchair—well, that doesn't exactly sound right. What I mean is, I assumed Tasha believed her wheelchair would be an issue, maybe a hindrance to things we could do if we started to spend more than computer time together. How could I inform her that I wanted to know everything about her without making her feel that her situation would scare me away? Because it wouldn't. The fact that she had endured such change in her life, and emerged such a true and positive Christian, drew me to her even more. And so I wrote:

> . . . I would love for you to share your story with me! I have been curious, but at the same time, since we've been just getting to know each other, I wanted you to feel comfortable telling me. I thought that when the time was right, you would share with me. I also thought about googling it last night when you mentioned that others had checked it out online, but decided that I wanted to hear it from you

instead. So please feel free to share with me anything that you would like to reveal about the accident and the time since then. And in return, I will share something with you today about my life . . . I'll start with the accident I referred to yesterday. As I mentioned, it turned out to be relatively minor, and I am blessed . . . but it changed me forever . . .

I took a chance. I shared my own car accident story, which happened during my days in Colorado, and resulted in no physical injury. I knew that my ignorance in high altitude mountain driving would pale by comparison. Yet I sensed that we shared similar outcomes . . . the incredible faith that grows from second chances.

I'll start with the accident. As I mentioned, it turned out to be fairly minor, but in retrospect, it could've been much, much worse. It was July 1999, and I was up in the mountains with a friend who came to visit me. There are certain mountains that are called "fourteeners" because the peak is over 14,000 feet up. Anyway, long story short, we had gone up one of them to about 12,500 feet when a storm started to brew. So we decided to head back down (there was a town at the bottom where we were going to have lunch). On the way down, I started to smell an odor like that of burning rubber, so I pulled over and put my car in park; I popped the hood and took a look. I could smell it but didn't see any smoke so didn't really think much of it. As soon as I put the car back into drive and tapped the brake pedal, it went to the floor and the car started rolling (as we were descending the mountain road). Immediately, I tried to put the car back into park, but of course, that didn't work. I tried to roll it into shrubbery, but that didn't work either. Before I knew it, we were gaining speed and heading down the road without brakes. My friend was yelling for us to jump, which I actually thought about, but didn't want to do. Eventually, we were up to about 45 mph and slowly gaining speed when I knew we were in serious trouble. As I rounded a curve in the road, it widened a bit so that there was a gravel shoulder on our side where the road seemed to level a bit. I had to take the shoulder because I was going so fast that I had no choice. My car did a 180, and before I knew it, was facing the direction we had just come from. Thankfully, doing the 180 caused my car to slow considerably, to the point where I could glance across the road and see not only a large, semi-flat grassy opening but a cluster of more sturdy trees. So I maneuvered the car to the other side (thankfully no cars coming up the other side of the road!) and was able to back it into a tree with minimal damage to my car, and no injuries to us. Very scary—I still remember my whole body shaking from fear. Literally seconds later, it started raining and hailing a bit as the storm came over. And if that wasn't enough to make me think that God was protecting me that day we had crashed in front of what looked like a camping area. We got out after the rain subsided and went to the front gate—the sign read "Christian Prayer Retreat Center"! Ever since that day I have firmly believed that God (and moreover the holy spirit) is walking beside me and saved me and my friend that day. I say that because after the tow truck came up, we discovered that my brake fluid had overheated, but I took the tow anyway, just to be safe. After we started down from there, I was looking around and there really wasn't anywhere else we could have safely stopped the car without crashing, flipping, or going down an embankment. We would've been over 50 mph by that point. I don't think about it too much anymore, but when I do, I still shudder at what could have happened if things had gone differently!

The other thing about my life that I'd like to share with you (quite different, but very personal nonetheless) has to do with my finances. I only share this now because I believe in being completely honest and upfront about anything and everything. You are someone who I'm really enjoying getting to know, and hope that it continues, but at the same time I feel that in order to really know me, this is important. It's not something that I'm ashamed about anymore (I was for a long time) because it defines where I came from, and the new me moving forward. In fact, it was shortly after this occurred that I rediscovered my relationship with Christ again. Two years ago this March I filed for bankruptcy due to a large accumulation of debt that I had. It's not that I was terrible with money (I rarely go out and buy anything fun for myself) but it was a combination of factors really that didn't work in my favor. It began when I took this job and discovered that my salary wasn't enough to really live on. I quickly fell behind on things like rent and bills (I had some minor credit cards bills that quickly got out of control within my first two years here). As time went on, I did get raises, and eventually a better salary when I was promoted to the head meteorologist, but by then, it was too late. After a few more years of struggle, I sought a financial counselor who advised me that filing for a bankruptcy was the only way to deal with this since my debt was substantial. It was in early 2010, when I was facing what would've been a catastrophic suit from one of my past creditors, that I was able to file. And it wasn't easy since I really couldn't afford the attorney's fee, but I believe that the spirit showed me a way, and I was able to make it happen two years ago March. In July 2010, it became final—my debts were discharged, and I've been debt-free ever since. In the past year and a half, I've been living on a strict budget where bills and essentials like food come first, with everything else secondary. I know it may sound elementary, but to me, that was a new beginning to my life. A second chance, if you will.

Less than one month after that final discharge, I was standing in my kitchen on a Saturday night feeling very lonely. Until that point, I had hidden that loneliness with things like friends and going out on Saturday nights till the wee hours to make myself feel liked and appreciated. Finally, that August night, the ultimate loneliness hit me like a hammer. I felt so separated from God—I hadn't been to church for several years, hadn't read his word, hadn't even prayed. But something inside of me was being stirred and I firmly believe the spirit was at work that night. I had remembered some people telling me about Jacob's Well a few years before, so I made the commitment that night that I would go the next morning. The year and a half since has been a complete life turnaround for me. I realized that God still loves me and hasn't forgotten about me, but I needed to go through some fire in my life to know that he's still working in me and wanted me back. My perspective on things, people, places, even music and TV shows has changed considerably.

I tell you all this, Tasha, because I want you to know that I have gone through some very low points in my life. But God has used those to make me stronger, more positive, and to rely on him more than ever. Whether our communication turns out to be a good friendship or if God has something more in store, I'm open to whatever his plan is. But I can honestly say that over these last couple of weeks, I see in you a heart for God and that is something special. I look forward to hearing your story, however much of it you care to share with me. I will return later to finish this, but I must go cook some food, or else I'll be a hungry guy later at work!! LOL . . . I hope you had a great day, Tasha, and I can't wait to hear from you again!

I was thrilled to hear back from Tasha. She agreed to share her story, which was essentially the first chapter of her soon-to-be-published book, *My Last Step Backward*. It was devastating to read, and it forced me to feel the fall as she dropped sixteen feet to a concrete basement floor. But the truth would build our relationship. And now, with the big stuff shared, we could focus on the future.

I had tried dating since "getting saved" . . . mostly girls who were not Christian at all. Every encounter brought the same revelation: so much of me had changed in a year. I had stopped going to bars. I was listening to different music. And now I wanted to complete my life change by spending my personal time with a woman who had the same Christian life that I did.

I felt more ready than ever to ask this amazing, resilient, and faith-filled woman out on a date. Our emails evolved into phone conversations.

Finally, in February, knowing Tasha was ready to meet, I popped the question.

CHAPTER FOUR

MINGLING WITH
THE EMAIL MAN

AFTER TEXTING AND TALKING on the phone for days, I realized I had met a true gentleman. He was not rushing anything. I began to wonder . . . *Hmm . . . is this a good thing? Should I worry that he hasn't pushed to meet me in person? Will we be Mingle pen pals forever?*

Angie wondered, too.

"Come on, Tasha. You two have to meet at some point! Think of the hours you spend reading his notes, planning your thoughts, and then writing your next message." It was true. I was meticulous about my messages and replies. In fact, Angie was one reason our email correspondence ended and we began talking on the phone instead. "You could make this a lot more efficient," she said, pointing out all of the time I spent every evening, painstakingly planning and composing my replies.

She was giving me good advice once again. "Just meet somewhere. Pick a spot halfway and see what you think!" My wise sister didn't have the patience for this cyber courtship.

And Doug was ready for the next step, too. In late January, he wrote:

. . . I wanted to bounce this off of you and see what you think. My ChristianMingle account (the emailing part) expires next week at the end of the month—originally I only signed up for one month. Since I can email you at your other address and you have mine, I was wondering what you thought about me doing that, rather than on here after next Tuesday. If you'd still rather go through Mingle email, then I'm just fine signing up for another month, but as you are the only one I'm interested in getting to know, I thought I'd see what your thoughts were.

I loved his last line. "Sure, cancel Mingle Mail." I wrote. "Our regular emails or the phone will work to keep in touch for now." . . . *Until we meet in person* . . . this last part was a thought only, but it was on my mind and in my heart around the clock.

My profile had indeed expired December 19, or so I thought. *Yes! It's shut down for good! I can't go back, even if I want to.*

But I kept getting emails! "Someone has sent you a message." "Someone sent you a smile."

They're just trying to lure me back in.

For twelve straight days, I noticed notification messages. *Why do I keep getting messages?* Finally, upon a closer look, I discovered my account had *not* expired.

I was so mad! ChristianMingle had simply charged my credit card for another three-month round. I didn't read the fine print and the site simply auto-enrolled me in a recurring membership. I would have to contact them.

That's when I saw Doug's smile.

Twelve days prior, on December 20, Doug had sent his attention-grabbing emoji. But it was January 1, and I thought maybe too much time had gone by. I felt like it was a waste of time.

Yet, before taking on ChristianMingle for a refund, I caught myself thinking, *I wonder what he said?* I thank God every day for my curiosity to click on his profile. And I thank ChristianMingle—now, I'm happy for their policy.

I SPENT FEBRUARY 6, Super Bowl Sunday, with my friends at church. While the guys were glued to the game, the girls visited at a table over a game of Skip-Bo. Somehow, the subject of Doug came up.

"He sounds great, Tasha. But how many weeks have you been talking? He needs to be brave and ask you out," one of the girls suggested.

"Yeah, we want to meet him," another friend added. "He could have been at this party today."

"Well, I don't think I'm ready for that," I said, waiting for my turn.

But in the midst of the card game, I actually felt a surge of confidence. I found myself wondering what was taking him so long. I knew, at this point, if he asked me out I would agree to meet him.

"Well, you sound ready for a date. So tell him to make a move, or he's gonna miss out!" one of my friends chimed in. "You can always go back to Mingle Mail to find a guy who's ready to ask you out on a proper date."

"He's probably dying to meet you," another offered. "Drop some hints! He might just be waiting for you to show that you're okay with it. That you're ready to meet."

I left the party appreciating my friends' support but knowing I could never suggest that we meet face-to-face. I made a twenty-first-century leap using the internet to meet this guy, but I was still very old-school about dating. Doug was going to have to ask me out.

And when I got home that evening, that's exactly what he did. I checked my phone and read his latest text:

"I don't want to pressure you, but I really want to set a time to meet."

Was he psychic? Had he somehow overheard our conversation? I was a little spooked, but I have to say, that's a text I will never forget!

"I have the next two Saturdays open. What works for you?" he asked.

That could mean less than a week to prepare. I wasn't sure if I could be ready. I was pondering my reply when my phone rang. I nearly jumped out of my wheelchair.

Peeking at caller ID, I saw it was Vernessa calling. "Hi, Vernessa. You're not going to believe this . . ."

I explained that I would likely respond to Doug with next Saturday.

"Next Saturday? Not this Saturday? Why wait? That will just drag things out. It's not like you two don't know each other. You've shared so many things online. So meet him!" Vernessa was pretty persuasive.

But I was suddenly a big chicken. I had instant fear . . . all of my confidence and smart talk over the Skip-Bo game had been sucked out by his text. Even though I had been very open and honest about my paralysis, I was concerned I hadn't given enough details about my limitations. Doug had finally asked me out, and I felt some of those old doubts creep back in.

"Two weeks out?! Tasha, you don't want to do that." Vernessa was making sense. "You'll get all nervous waiting around. Just get past the anxiety of meeting. Take it from me, the sooner, the better."

"But I need a haircut! I need to go shopping. I need a full makeover!" My insecurities were peaking at this point.

"Ha! You? A makeover? That would be the day. He could pop in on you first thing in the morning, and he'd say, 'Wow, she's gorgeous!'"

Saturday, February 11, six days from his text. I couldn't believe I agreed to this! I replied, and then devoted the entire week to getting ready for this first date.

Caregivers helped me select my outfit. Not too heavy with the sweater. Sure, winter weather was an issue, but I didn't want to look like a woolly mammoth, wrapped in a shag rug. I also didn't want my teeth chattering the whole time. No short sleeves, even though I did prefer my summer colors. I visualized my favorite tops in the closet, pastels, usually sleeveless. Rats! It was February!

I searched for a weather forecast on my phone. The high on Saturday: eleven degrees!

RACHEL CAME OVER THE night before I met Doug. Lord knows I needed a good massage to work out the stress in my neck and shoulders from all this date tension.

"So are you still talking with—what was his name—Doug? Wasn't that your online Mingle Man?" Of course she remembered. Rachel doesn't forget a thing.

"Yes, it's Doug—and I'm meeting him tomorrow for the first time. I'm so scared!" Rachel thought she could make me feel better about this, but it backfired.

"Bring up his profile again." We were in my office, my chair parked in front of my computer. "Oh my gosh, Tasha. He is so good looking!" Rachel was right, but this actually added to my anxiety. Why would a handsome guy like this be interested in me? "Look at those muscles! He must work out all the time." Rachel's massage therapy was only one aspect of her holistic career in wellness. She had a fitness degree as well—you couldn't fool Rachel. She could tell when people just naturally looked healthy and when they truly lived the lifestyle, like she did. I was excited that she approved of Doug's dedication to weight training and fitness. But this made my fears grow even more. We were very different people, and he would know after one date that his dedication to working out couldn't be shared by me. I would never be going to head to the gym with him. In my mind, I was dumped before date number two.

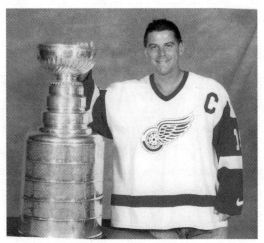

One of Doug's ChristianMingle profile pictures—posing with the traveling Stanley Cup.

And if I wasn't dumped, what was the catch? This was too good to be true. I had prayed for months, but would God come through now? I just couldn't believe this was all that it seemed. *Anxiety! Stop!*

"What? Is that hurting you?" Rachel asked.

Oops. I must have said "stop" out loud.

"No, sorry. You're fine. That feels great." *But I'm canceling my date,* I thought.

I didn't share this idea with Rachel, however. I knew she would throw Beth Moore into this.

Beth Moore, the founder of Living Proof Ministries for Women and the author of numerous faith-based books, wrote something that changed me forever. It became a sort of treatise for personal strength and independence during that stretch between the bad breakup and Doug—a book I'll probably never stop consulting.

So Long, Insecurity: You've Been a Bad Friend to Us taught me so many lessons. It saved my life from dark doubts about being single, about thinking only women dealt with insecurities. This book gave me courage to face life without couplehood. Yet, at the same time, once I met Doug, it reminded me not to slip into the fears and doubts that can destroy relationships before they ever get a solid start.

If there is one book that helped me grow and confront the adult world of work, relationships, and faith, *So Long, Insecurity* was it. And Rachel knew it. She had an uncanny ability to sense my mental worries as she massaged the physical tension from my limbs. She had more than once said, "Where's that Beth Moore book? I think we need her, right here, right now!"

I was going to call Doug to cancel as soon as Rachel left. Then I remembered my caregiver was coming to put me to bed. I would do it in the morning. We were planning on meeting at three o'clock at Caribou Coffee in Menomonie. It was a fifty-minute drive. I would have time in the morning to text him and cancel, and he'd still be able to salvage his day.

Call. Text. Get out of it! All night long, I conducted an inner war. I coached myself on what to say. After morning cares, I motored to my bathroom mirror. *You don't have enough makeup on. What does it matter; you aren't going!*

"Britney, will you come in here? I think I need more makeup." *Beth Moore would be appalled,* I thought.

My caregiver must have thought I was crazy! Twenty minutes later, after another battle—should I go? *No, I'm canceling. Call him now. No! Wait another hour.* I called out again. "Britney, I have too much makeup on. Will you help me?"

The what-ifs raced in and out all morning, reminding me of my old boyfriend's complaints. "Do you know how lucky you are to have me? There's not another guy in the world who would do what I do for you." When he got angry, sick of helping me, and impatient with my pace in life, I blamed myself. I would find myself apologizing and agreeing.

As I debated over this first date with Doug, I know that I was still recovering from the damage and still wondering if the last guy was right. I was thinking that a date with Doug Michaels was going to lead to one of two things anyway—either another painful relationship like the last, or him hightailing it after a brief date and never being heard of again.

What is the point of all this? Why bother? I'll get back to dedicating my life to work and avoid these emotionally painful highs and lows. I don't have time for these drama games that end in heartache anyway. Didn't I vow after the last one never to put myself through this again?

As I battled between tears of fear and the excitement of meeting someone who might change my life forever, my inner monologue could not tell time.

If I don't get going right now, I'm gonna be late! There are winter roads to deal with. Start warming up the van. It's too late to cancel now! I have to go!

I should have left at two. By now it was two thirty. *Is it too late to cancel? Can I still send him a message?*

This was not my voice this time. Not my inner monologue. I have never heard God's voice audibly, but I knew His message: *Tasha, get in the van. You need to go. Tasha, when have I ever failed you?*

My faith started after my accident. It grew with my understanding that life was better from this altered perspective and that life had no limits with my new limitations. Once I accepted Him into my life, my worries were under His control. I slipped and forgot this from time to time. Not a full step backward, just a loss of balance, let's say. When I heard God's reminder to trust in Him again, I listened!

God knows, I needed him now more than ever! Would Doug Michaels wait for me? I was certain to be late! It was a clear day, with icy patches along State Highway 63. I would have to make up time on the freeway.

I was definitely driving too fast to text or call. Pulling over to contact him would slow me down even more! I worried now that he was going to leave.

You've never failed me, you've never failed me! I was repeating this phrase to God, not my van. Yet, at 80 mph, even the Courage Center would have revoked my license had they found out the speed in which I traveled that day.

At a table in Caribou Coffee, Doug Michaels indeed began to worry. I eventually asked him, "Did you think you were being stood up?"

"Well, yes. The thought crossed my mind. But honestly, I was more worried about your driving than anything." Ironic! This was the start of a lifelong concern for his wife's driving. Because of my van's conversion, uniquely customized for me, for a long time Doug couldn't say, "Hey, you seem tired, Tasha. Pull over. Let me drive."

Doug had his own set of what-ifs going on, which he later told me. *What kind of van allows a quadriplegic to drive on I-94? What if she has an accident? Maybe I should have offered to drive to Ellsworth or River Falls—somewhere closer?*

Finally, I pulled into the parking lot and there he was, waiting for me. This was surreal. He had noticed my van driving up, left his table, and come out to greet me. He was waiting for me!

"God will do abundantly more than you could dare ask or think." Ephesians 3:20. At my friend Ryan's wedding, this was the reading we heard. I attended with Vernessa and listened closely. I knew the depth of Ryan's faith and understanding. It gave me hope that if God gave him the opportunity to find and marry the love of his life that maybe I would find the same blessing. With Doug's greeting, I was beginning to find it truly possible.

I often reminisced about Ryan's wedding and how happy I was for him, yet it was hard to witness. He had called me the December before to say he was going to ask Julie. This was the height of my own period of doubt. I had the antithesis of personal happiness. I wanted the best for him, but his wedding was a reminder that others were moving forward in their personal happiness. I felt stalled, broken down, with a perpetual flat tire.

I thought of Ryan's genuine look of bliss as he watched while Julie walked down the aisle. Then Ryan's face faded as I rolled out of my van and into the coffee shop with someone who was arguably the most handsome man I had ever met.

Doug, like me, ordered hot chocolate. "I've probably had enough coffee for the day," he said. We luckily found a table despite the busy atmosphere. I chose Caribou for a few reasons. First, I wanted to have a social drink, one that would keep me from shivering on a cold winter's day. Secondly, I didn't want to eat in front of Doug.

I can handle a thermal mug. I always bring my own, a style that is easy for a weak grip to handle. But eating required my tenodesis splint—a teno, as I call it. If you have ever attended one of my presentations, or if you've read my first book, you know the love-hate relationship I have with this apparatus that provides a grip for a very paralyzed hand. Holt, my friend who is paralyzed due to a hockey accident, talked me into trying it. Barb, the best occupational therapist on earth, trained me in. It is on my list of essential tools for mobility. But I call it the Terminator hand for a reason. This unattractive attachment is the last thing I wanted my date to see! However, I didn't want to be fed by a caregiver, so I learned years ago that this ugly splint is really a beautiful invention. I had brought it along since Doug had mentioned in his text that dinner might be a part of the date-plan.

"If all goes well, let's stick around and find a place for supper—make an evening of it. If for any reason you don't like me," he stated, "I'll let you go on your way. You are free to end our date, and don't feel obligated to meet or talk with me again."

I was convinced it would be the other way around, that he wouldn't like me. My online pictures can't begin to show the depth of my disability. How could this handsome man think that I would reject him?

"What makes you think that I will be the one to call this quits after one hot chocolate?"

His answer is precisely why I knew in my heart I should meet this man . . . he had me with this reply:

"Oh, I know I will like you. I already do. This is not my worry. But if you decide you don't like me, I want you to have an out."

I couldn't believe my ears.

"So," he continued. "If you like me, let's have dinner. And keep next Saturday open, too."

My inner monologue went to, *Thank you, God. He appears to be all that I anticipated and more.*

While I was trying to dress for winter yet not come completely lost in layers of fabric, Doug clearly had a different plan. Within minutes, he took off his jacket to reveal a set of biceps—displayed quite nicely in his American Eagle T-shirt. *No Photoshop,* I thought. *That picture was the real deal.*

In the blink of an eye, three hours raced by. I can't tell you what we talked about; all I know is that the sun was going down.

We talked nonstop, with balanced contributions to the discussion, and suddenly it was six o'clock.

"So," Doug interrupted. "It's your call. Do you want to have dinner? Should we find a restaurant?"

He'll have to see your teno . . . Say no. Say no!

"Sure." I smiled as he put on his jacket.

"Let's just make our way across the parking lot to Applebee's," Doug stated. He pointed and continued. "See it over there? In fact, why don't I just hop in your van? That's okay, isn't it?"

My new van was a beauty I'd been driving since December 27. Just getting the thing started felt new and awkward. I resisted my instinct to say, "Take your own car."

"Sure. Let's go."

That night with Doug, I was still learning to place the key in the ignition of this new van—something most drivers do without thinking. Just finding the slot proved a slow challenge, an awkward action I wasn't sure I wanted Doug to see. And yet he didn't seem bothered by this delay—except for the fact that he was freezing. Perhaps he should have covered those guns with a sweater under his coat. I was laughing at his chattering teeth, but now believe this was the only time we shared the same body temp. Freeze Baby remains my nickname, while Doug walks around our house in tank tops and shorts, even in January!

When we finally rolled into the next parking lot, it was six thirty on a Saturday night, and the Applebee's was packed. "Wow, not one parking spot," I stated.

"Yeah. Every handicapped spot is full," Doug echoed. "Well, there's always Pizza Hut." Doug was hungry. The sugar had worn off.

"Great idea!" As expected, the Pizza Hut parking was wide open. We still have a fondness for this place. So quietly deserted, it's an intimate place to eat.

Back at Caribou Coffee, a nice-looking young woman had greeted Doug as she passed our table. "Hey, Doug."

"Oh, hi, Lisa."

I only mention this because of the fact that it happened again at Pizza Hut. Even with so few diners, Doug was noticed. The only other couple in the restaurant spoke up as they exited. "Hey, aren't you Doug Michaels?" When Doug pleasantly affirmed this, the man asked, "Isn't this weather crazy?"

Wow, this is a switch. I'm so used to people recognizing me. My story was well known in western Wisconsin and the Twin Cities. Area newspapers and TV stations had faithfully followed up on me, especially at milestone anniversaries of my accident. Having my story morph into a career as a speaker had increased the likeliness that people in this part of the world will recognize me. But this time, the roles were reversed. Tasha Schuh would not get all of the attention while out with this media man.

Surprisingly, I liked it!

When our order was delivered to the table, Doug instantly began to eat, commenting on how good it was. With my splint on my lap, I debated whether I should try eating without the aid of my teno.

Between his bites, I warned Doug of what he was about to see . . .

"That looks yummy! Hey, Doug, I have this splint I have to wear in order to eat."

He continued to chew. With his mouth full, he appeared to have a revelation. "Oh, sorry. Do you need help putting it on?"

"No," I answered. "But, I thought maybe I could get by without it tonight . . ." Doug was into his second piece now. "Looks like I'm going to have to put it on."

Brief pause in his chewing.

"I hope you don't mind," I said.

"What? No. Of course not. You'd better dig in, or you're not gonna get a piece."

I was beginning to really like this guy. He was pigging out, and I swear, if I hadn't said anything, he wouldn't have taken a breath from eating to even notice my teno.

I should have been hungry, but with all the hot chocolate and a nervous date-stomach, I barely had room for food. I forced myself to eat two pieces. When Doug appeared to be finished, he leaned in and pointed at the last slice, "Can I have this?"

"Sure," I laughed. He was a bottomless pit!

Actually, I was thrilled that he seemed so himself—so comfortable eating his fill in front of me. In some ways, this did not feel like a first date at all. We were old friends finally catching up with each other after weeks of emails.

We finished our meal, then laughed and talked and lingered. Time stood still for us, and since the restaurant wasn't busy, the staff didn't seem bothered that we showed no signs of leaving, even after our table was cleared. I looked down at the time on my phone.

"It's nine!" My caregiver was scheduled to come at ten, and we were still sitting in the restaurant!

We headed for the van, and I had even more trouble with the key for my ignition. Doug started shivering like a little schoolgirl on the bus.

"Yeah! I'm not the only freeze baby!" I announced.

I often remind Doug of this wintery first date. "You lied to me that night. You looked like you hated winter. You love the cold! I thought I was hooking up with my ticket to the Sunbelt, but I was conned!"

I returned him to his car so I could jump on the road home.

No hug and no kiss, but we made plans for our next date! Saturday—one week away. Same time, same place!

I quickly called my caregiver. "I'm late!" I said in my voice message. "Don't go to my house! I won't get there until . . ."

Fortunately, she arrived right when I got home.

SO THIS WAS THE START of it all—our whirlwind romance, which led to a year of commutes on I-94 and endless correspondence. We talked every day! Doug called during his break at work, which was sometime between the six and ten o'clock news. In the early stages, I would text him good-night just as a caregiver was putting me to bed. By midyear, we were talking on the phone after work, too, into the wee hours of the morning.

Sleep is overrated when you're in love.

Goofing around on a date in Winona, MN.

CHAPTER FIVE

HOW DISABLED HANDS GOT A GRIP ON MY MAN

DOUG WILL DEFINITELY SPEAK to this topic. Who knows better than he why an active, healthy man felt compelled to meet and pursue a relationship with someone so limited by paralysis? I told Rachel way back in the Mingle Mail stage, "This guy is different." But I didn't know how different—how special—until we started to spend time like a regular couple. We took a rather abnormal dating situation and made it our new normal. And this was quite a leap, since it involved a wound vacuum and an unladylike suction sound that mimicked flatulence at its best!

Let's back up to late January, just prior to the Super Bowl Sunday party. I had met a brutally honest doctor at Gillette Hospital who had lost hope in my home remedies for a rather large skin wound on my left hip. This was not a pressure sore, but a nagging, chronic wound resulting from trauma due to a bumpy wheelchair ride during a summer music festival in South Dakota the previous July. I was doing my usual—underplaying just how deep this opened wound was. I resisted my doctor's recommendation to give in and check out of life for six weeks to heal properly. I had a cluttered calendar of speaking events and now hope for more dates with Doug Michaels.

"Six weeks in a hospital room, off your seat, and in a special bed—that's the only way to get this under control."

"Well, there's got to be a plan B. I'm not going to the hospital."

I could be so stubborn when I wanted something. It's funny how Old Tasha—the strong-willed teenager who wanted the part of Sandy in *Grease* in the worst way—would rear her stubborn head and demand another option. I conferenced with Angie, who concurred: pray for a miracle and use the wound vacuum. But I should go about my normal business.

The wound vac was a built-in suction apparatus designed to accelerate the healing process. It accompanied me in my wheelchair and spouted off gurgling noises at the most inopportune times—like on a date.

"Yeah, I think I heard some strange noises," Doug admits when asked about it now. "But I thought it was your wheelchair. That thing has so many bells and whistles. I figured any odd noises had something to do with your chair."

But Angie would remind me, "You sound like you have gas. He's gonna find out. Just tell him what you're dealing with."

"No!" I replied.

I didn't want to scare him off before he really got to know me. This was not a part of my normal life. Out of all the years I had been sitting in my wheelchair, this marked the first time I needed a medical device like this. It didn't feel necessary to tell him about something so temporary. This would heal. Things would quiet down. Literally. I just needed a little more time.

But quite the opposite occurred. The wound got worse and the harsh doctor got his way. By mid-March, he refused my pleas to try something else at home.

"Tasha, I can feel your hip bone when I place my finger inside this wound. Your infected hip bone. You don't have a choice any longer. Go home. Cancel your presentations. Pack a few things. I want you back at this hospital for six weeks. We're going at this with everything we've got now."

"I do not have six weeks!" I replied. "My life is very busy."

"What's the big deal? How full can your calendar be?" my doctor asked. His words stung, and then my tears began to flow right there in the clinic. This was sometimes the tone I felt from others when I voiced how busy I was with work. Not everyone. But people who didn't really know me, who didn't comprehend the hours, the maneuvering, the perseverance it took to build a professional calendar of speaking events. I read my doctor's urging as, "It's wonderful that the disabled girl feels needed, but right now she has to heal." As if the contracts I had were probably favors to keep the ambitious young woman in the wheelchair busy. The body language implied, "People will understand when you cancel. You can be replaced."

The PA, the physician's assistant who had been following me since the onset of this wound, understood. She knew about Doug and all of the schedule rearranging I would have to do, and she hugged me.

"So where's the awesome attitude I always see, Tasha? You can do this." She comforted me, but knew this had to happen.

This is when I felt disabled, but not by my chair. By my inability to convey that my business mattered. I mattered. I would be missed at these presentations. And sure, it was a lost opportunity for me, but this was a loss to an audience as well. Each group would miss a chance to hear my unique story. I felt as if this doctor didn't understand the value of sharing my story and the many ways that my sharing it could help people. I resented my doctor's tone the day he ordered me into the hospital, but there wasn't a thing I could do about it. Regardless of how relentless I had been to develop and expand my business, I would now have to cancel everything and lie helpless in a bed thinking about all I would miss.

I went home and cried for six hours straight.

Angie would again come to my rescue. I called her in tears just as I was leaving the clinic. She consoled me and we hung up as I started my drive home. What an inconvenience this must have been for the mom of three busy girls. But when I arrived back at my house, Angie was already in my driveway.

"Talk to me."

I couldn't. I tried, but I could not stop my tears.

"Slow down. This is more than just work . . . more than just calendar changes."

She knew me better than anyone. "What's really wrong?"

Finally, I spit out his name through my sobs. "Doouggg!"

I was very upset about losing the work and canceling presentations. But there was no point in trying to fool Angie; 90 percent of why I was so upset was Doug.

"Well, what about Doug?" Angie asked. My sobs startled Lily, one of my cats. She retreated to my bedroom.

I gasped for air like a swimmer in deep water for too long, emerging to find enough O_2 to utter a sentence.

"The second I tell him, he's gone!" I sputtered.

"What?" Angie questioned. "Why would you jump to this? Think about it, Tasha. Would you leave? Would you say, 'Bye-bye, guy,' if the tables were turned and Doug had to be admitted into the hospital?"

I didn't know how to reply. "Well, would you?" Angie pressed the issue.

"No. But I'm a girl," was my wet and sloppy rebuttal.

"What difference does that make?" Angie's logic usually won when we argued like this, but all my insecurities would surface before I backed down that day.

"Women are programmed to help with things like this. We just want to be there."

"Well, that's just crazy talk. Would Scott bail if I needed to stay in the hospital for weeks?"

"That's not a fair comparison." Scott was not only a loyal husband but also the father of three daughters. He had plenty of practice accommodating the women in his life, starting way back in 1997 with a visit to my Rochester ICU room the night of my accident.

"Well, what will his mom think?" More tears fell as I spoke. Angie handed me another tissue.

"Who? Doug's mom? How can you know, Tasha? You haven't even met her yet."

Angie was right. Doug had asked that we ease into our relationship when it came to family. I understood completely why he was reserved, and I cared about his parents' approval of me. Most moms probably would have reservations about their son dating someone who appeared to have so many limitations. I had met many of Doug's close friends during our early months together, but maybe the parents of an only child would be confused, even upset by his choice to spend time with someone so differ-ent—so opposite of who they must have envisioned for him. Why involve them if this wasn't a lasting thing? And at this point I feared it wasn't.

"I just think that this is a deal breaker." I truly believed that I was betray-ing Doug by having to leave, for medical reasons, at this crucial point in our relationship.

"What are you talking about? People go into the hospital for all kinds of reasons, Tasha—even nondisabled people. No one can guarantee that they won't get sick or hurt and need medical help." Angie was not buying into all my worries. But after a few hospital stays, I had learned which friends could persevere with me and which could not.

I had devoted our first months together to proving just how easy this was—how paralysis was no big deal. Would Doug think I lied to him? Misled him into thinking I could facilitate life with paralysis the same way, or maybe even better, than most women he would meet? He deserved to end it all. A deal breaker—this was truly a deal breaker.

After challenging every single one of my insecurities, Angie finally ended with, "I think you are going to be surprised. I think Doug is different, and special, and really cares about you."

Angie left. Mom called. She was on her way to help me get things in or-der. Thank goodness Beth Moore is now on my Kindle. I need to reread! Again! Insecurity stinks! I hadn't felt this emotionally weak in months.

I talked with my dad as well and informed him of the hospital plans. But then an unexpected call came from Pastor Ted Marsh, my friend and spiritual dad. He and my friend Jan O'Meara were like having another set of parents. Pastor Ted, who knew Doug quite well already, stated on the phone with full confidence, "Doug will be all right. You just take care of you."

Pastor Ted, who treated me like a daughter, had called Doug up not long after our first Caribou Coffee encounters.

"You know I have to do this, Tasha. I have to take him out for lunch."

"I know. Thanks for looking out for me." I made no objection and only hoped that Doug would not be offended by this request.

I found out later that Doug welcomed the invitation to an Eau Claire cafe, and thanked Pastor Ted for "caring so much about Tasha." Ted had called me the next day with, "He's a good guy, Tasha. He's genuine. In fact, I gotta tell you, the first time you brought him to church, I just kept a watchful eye on him. And his eyes were glued to you the whole time. His interest is in you. He's sincere."

Pastor Ted's call helped. I got busy again at my computer, making calls and clearing my calendar, when Doug texted me.

Doug: "How was your day?"

Me: "Not good."

Bringggg! The phone rang immediately.

"What do you mean, not good? Tasha, this isn't you. You never have a negative thing to say. What's going on?" Doug was genuinely concerned.

I leveled with him and told the truth. "So now I'm stuck in a hospital bed for six weeks. I have the pageant coming up, the book to finish, my calendar events to cancel—but the hardest thing is not seeing you."

Doug's reaction was so understated. It was like the whole teno thing again. No big deal. No worries.

"I can visit you, right?"

"Well, yes, but I have to decide if I should go to Rochester or to St. Paul."

Doug helped me make that decision. If the level of care would be equal, why not go to Gillette?

"St. Paul is only another twenty minutes on I-94, not much further than what I've been driving. Rochester's not as convenient. So, if you're going to get the same results, why not be a little closer?"

I loved that he was willing to plan this with me. He shocked me when he said he would plan to spend weekends at Gillette.

"Behave during the week. Get some book stuff done. Then we can hang out, watch TV, talk—pretty much do the same stuff we've been doing at your house most Saturdays and Sundays, right?"

My confidence climbed out of the dark hole I had dug from doubts and past worries of what boyfriends do when faced with adversity. But Doug was like no boyfriend I had ever had. By the end of that phone call, I had put myself back together, canceled events, and made up my mind I would be discharged in record time. I had a national pageant to prepare for, a book coming out, and Doug, all within reach. I was not about to take six weeks respite time with so much pending.

With prayer and compliance, I set a goal to heal much faster than planned. Oddly enough, my hospital room proved to be a couple's retreat. It was a strange way to build a relationship, but once Doug offered to spend the weekends at the hospital, I knew there was hope that I would be discharged with boyfriend still intact.

Doug drove from Eau Claire that very first Saturday. I had one of my personal caregivers come do my hair and makeup. The hospital accepted my request to have my own personal staff for certain aspects of my daily routine. I didn't want to just lay them off for the duration of my hospital stay, and who knew my private routines better than they did? For cares related to my healing, the hospital nurses were fabulous. Like my sand bed. This high-tech mattress kept me floating on air, or so it seemed. Precautions related to this, or any of my vital indicators regarding the healing process, remained in Gillette's hands. But "regular" cares required throughout this hospital stay could be completed by my personal caregivers.

For example, my more private tasks included my bowel care program which was too lengthy and difficult for others to complete. The Gillette nurses were willing to learn, but from past experiences in hospital stays, I knew that I wanted my own caregivers who were trained and could spend the full hour that I needed for this. On Sundays, Tuesdays, and Thursdays two caregivers drove together to Gillette from Ellsworth. Then, early Saturday morning, they returned again to prep for Doug! There was no way he was seeing me without makeup! On one of our dates, he commented on how he looked forward to when he could see me without makeup. *Never!* I thought. We laugh about that now.

One caregiver in particular—she was the best with my bowel care program—couldn't drive. So she caught a ride with another member of my home staff. One girl primped me for my "date" after my bowel care expert did my personal cares.

Flat in bed for weeks meant I had to eat, swallow my pills, and visit with Doug without lifting my head, neck, or shoulders off the sand mattress that sustained me in a pressure-free position. I remember thinking, *I don't want Doug to feed me.* So I got pretty creative when it came to getting enough high-protein calories in me for cell growth and healing. I wanted some semblance of independence, not to fool Doug but to match his amazing attitude that this was not that big a deal.

I had the nurse on duty camouflage my room. Hide the catheters! Clear the counter of tubes and bandages! I didn't want to look sick . . . just nursing a little annoyance. I feared that the fastest way to turn a boyfriend off was to reveal all the responsibilities that come with quadriplegia. I wanted Doug to see a calm, cool, collected Tasha.

This is a minor setback. The doctor is making a big deal out of nothing was the impression I wanted to convey to Doug—and is, in fact, the reality I create every time I have a medical setback. Dad's nickname for me at times like this: Moses. I would part the seas; I would work a miracle. What is all the fuss about? As far as I was concerned, Doug would see me on a mini vacation—an antiseptic respite.

While visiting that first Saturday, Doug asked, "So can I just stay here next weekend—overnight? Skip the late-night driving and spend more time with you. I'd like to get back to Eau Claire for service at Jacob's Well Sunday morning. But that's not until ten forty-five. I could have breakfast with you and then take off."

I loved this offer. My faith that Doug wanted a serious relationship with me as much as I wanted one with him grew from this request. Yet I feared he would find out more than I wanted him to know about my condition. Would he see the worries and medical madness that sometimes come with being so different and then decide this was too much for him?

Once again, Joni Eareckson Tada's book reminded me about the importance of confidence. *Choices, Changes* describes Joni as so absorbed in her first date with Ken Tada, the man who would become her husband, she forgot to empty her leg bag. She didn't shield Ken from this. She didn't end the date abruptly. Instead, Joni asked Ken to empty the bag for her!

Tasha, be like Joni! Didn't Joni want Ken to see everything? I need to be like that! If Doug can't handle it, he's not the right man for me.

I soon began to coin this as my "Joni confidence."

There was only one way to answer Doug's question: let him stay, let Doug see, but not see, what it took to heal a wound that was all too common for someone with my disability. In other words, I would welcome him into my room, into my world of quadriplegia, to potentially witness all the trials and tribulations that accompany this condition. But I would facilitate my own healing with such ease. I would avoid drama and accept help with grace and appreciation so that he witnessed, firsthand, this big deal was not a big deal at all.

And in my desire to create levity from loss, I gained. I healed in two-thirds of the time my doctor predicted. Instead of six weeks, I took four. And, best of all, I fell in love with Doug in the process.

Doug came every weekend during my stay at Gillette. A kind nurse rolled a sleep-recliner into the room, and Doug never complained, even though Mom and Jan Omeara had commented they needed a chiropractor after sleeping on it.

Doug and I watched videos—my classic film picks, like *Tommy Boy* and *Hitch*, and his favorite TV series, *Home Improvement*. We would be laughing so hard that the nurses would pop in. I think they wanted in on our fun.

"Are you sure you are okay in here? We can hear Doug laughing all the way down the hall," one nurse said as she entered to check in.

By the beginning of my fourth week of stay, I had graduated to fifteen-minute increments sitting in a chair. By the middle of that week, we were planning my discharge.

Ironic as it sounds, this was a joyful time. I made it my mission to go in with a good attitude, focusing on being a light in my nurses' lives, and I could not believe how fast the time went! It felt like I blinked and I was leaving. This was a huge lesson in my life. Life is what we make it. I thought about all of the meals, cards, visitors, and prayers that I could feel from all who pulled for me, and they told me again I was blessed by God's grace. As many tears as I shed going into the hospital, I actually cried when I left.

I was overwhelmed by the wonderful people I met, especially one CNA who told me on my final day how much I impacted her and the entire staff.

"We don't want you to leave," she stated on her last shift with me. "Before you came, I was really questioning what my purpose was. I can't thank you enough for all our talks."

She was young, and she didn't know what her next step in life would be. I remember chatting with her and letting her know that everything would work out. She just needed to be reminded that her future was so bright, and she should be excited about the possibilities. I don't know where she is today, but there's no doubt in my mind that she is helping people.

I recall my doctor trying to warn me as I prepared for discharge, "You know, this is new skin. Patients who go home too early sometimes come right back with the same problem—or worse."

"I'm not coming back," I said firmly. And I didn't. I took his warning seriously, but I knew I would take every precaution to avoid a bounce-back. I had too many incentives to stay safe and healthy.

Number one was an attentive, handsome man with whom I had become very close during my stay at Gillette. Doug's commute to see me on the weekends was again reduced now that I was discharged and home, providing even more time together.

It was about this time that Doug began offering to do some of my cares—or at least the ones that would give us a little more privacy.

For instance, Doug learned to transfer me. He could lift me from my chair to the sofa pretty easily. And since my sitting hours were limited right after hospital discharge, transfers were more frequent. Thus, when Doug came on the weekends, my caregivers could make fewer stops at the house, which meant fewer interruptions.

Although it was Doug who brought up the sleeping arrangements before I had a chance to voice my opinion.

"If I am going to spend nights here, I am sleeping in the guest bedroom, Tasha."

"Good. I agree. I wasn't sure what you were thinking . . ." I was relieved he took the lead on this. If he wasn't going to share this with me, I had already planned to bring it up. We had exactly the same "arrangements" in mind—another sign we were meant for each other.

"I've decided that if this is meant to be, I'm waiting until our wedding night to be intimate," Doug explained. "There're plenty of examples to prove that waiting is worth it, and plenty of examples to prove that not waiting hurts a relationship."

Clearly, we were talking about the most private of things—the most intimate details. Yet, he still hadn't asked me about my bathroom cares. He still didn't know that I had my bladder re-routed to my belly button—so that I could insert a catheter to empty my bladder without getting undressed.

Angie and Melissa both inquired, "Have you told him yet? Or are you chicken?"

"I'm not chicken. I want him to ask me." I replied.

Angie's theory was, "He's probably googled it. You might as well tell him."

But if he had googled it, I figured that would have prompted him to ask.

My gut instinct was that he didn't know. And over time, I discovered that I was right. Doug still had lots to learn about me.

CHAPTER SIX

COUPLEHOOD

PEOPLE HAVE OFTEN COMMENTED, "Your courtship was pretty fast and furious." We did indeed start talking about being together forever after only a few months of dating. We often face questions like, "What made you both know this was 'the one'?"

We both agree that honesty was present from the start. I may have tried to shelter Doug from the full extent of my condition. But that was never to be dishonest—only intended to show how manageable my "different" life was, as if I were saying, "I got this."

I wish I had saved my ChristianMingle profile, but all of my writings disappeared with my account cancellation once I gave up the site to correspond solely with Doug. Yet I know for a fact that I didn't hide my disability. I might have been insecure about my ability to attract the right man, but firm in this: if my disability deterred someone, I was not interested in him anyway.

I didn't overemphasize my disability either. I am so much more than a paralyzed person dependent upon a wheelchair. Just like my hospital stay didn't have to accentuate the burden of healing, I have always tried to show the truth about my "different" way of life without making it seem too difficult.

For instance, Doug will acknowledge that he saw my disabled hands in my profile picture, but will also tell you he did not notice they were relatively useless. He saw the word "paralyzed" in my write-up and my body in the expensive motorized chair, but he saw past the limited limbs. I believe a genuine smile has something to do with this. And although my mobility is slower, I take pride in fluid movement that is graceful and natural. In fact, all blind dates should take a lesson in slowing things down to really look at the person; listen to his voice; and see, hear, and sense all you are getting yourself into. It reveals the truth about who you are meeting and sends red flags if you need them, and if things are right, you will observe special qualities about this person that you perhaps would miss if you were dating at the traditional pace.

I truly think that my disability gave some men a reason to think that I would lower my standards to date them, that there's a level of desperation that occurs when something is "wrong" or different about you. Many men who should have been working on their own self-improvement reached out to me. I wanted to say, "Sorry. I'll pray for you, but I am not dating you." (I thank God for the delete button.)

I meant it when I said in my profile, "I love God, and I'm very passionate about His purpose for my life. If you don't agree with that, please don't contact me." Since Doug said, and meant, the same thing, we could embark on a pretty fast and efficient path to knowing one another.

Doug gets all of the credit for how quickly I learned to trust his sincere desire to know the real Tasha Schuh.

Shortly after discharge from the hospital, still on a strict seating schedule, we spent a few hours out at my sister's home for my niece's birthday party. For a long time, all of Angie's girls had a passion for American Girl dolls. For months, my niece Anna begged for the wheelchair that could be purchased as an accessory for her doll. Obviously, I was excited to get this for her—the perfect gift! So, the day of, when she opened it, we saw the reaction we anticipated; she was thrilled! I didn't think much about it, since this was the reaction I was shooting for—this was what she wanted.

When Doug and I got back to my house, Doug seemed really quiet. He had something on his mind.

"Are you okay?" I asked. "Is everything alright?"

He took a moment. When I looked over at him, I could see that his eyes had welled up with tears.

"Your niece, her favorite gift was a wheelchair!" He was having a hard time finding his words. "That's a symbol of sadness, depression. What ten-year-old wants this? Most kids are looking for video games or some really expensive toy. I guess I just haven't seen anything like this. Your family, Tasha, look how much you've influenced their thinking on this."

I guess that I hadn't even thought about the symbolism of this. By the time we had left Angie's house, my nieces were all fighting over this toy. It was normal for us.

This was the first time I saw Doug cry. This showed me how much he was soaking in all of this—all of my world. And it showed what a kind heart Doug had. He and I wonder whether there is a part of his capacity to empathize—to feel for others—that he just wouldn't have experienced if he hadn't come into my world.

THE NEXT EVENT THAT helped me realize that Doug was in this for real was Vernessa's wedding.

After only two dates with Doug, we were texting quite regularly. And one evening, after spending the day bridesmaid dress shopping with Vernessa, I made the biggest dating gaffe of them all. I asked Doug to be my date to Vernessa's wedding!

What did I just do? It was true—I had just committed the greatest faux pas of them all. But it was impossible to take back a text. Our conversation started quite innocently:

Doug texted first: *How was your day?*

I replied: *Great! Vernessa and I went dress shopping for her wedding. It's going to be beautiful!*

Doug texted again: *Sounds like fun!*

My reply: *It will be! Wanna go?*

Seconds felt like minutes—hours, even! *Oh, no! He's trying to think of a way to turn me down! Why did I text that without thinking? We've hardly spent any time together, and I just asked him to a friend's wedding?*

Doug's reply, moments later: *I'd love to!*

Whew! Panic mode deterred.

I didn't want Doug to feel pressured into going to Vernessa and David's wedding. Yet by the time the event rolled around—Memorial Day weekend—we had been dating for some months, and he seemed genuinely excited to attend.

Certainly, an event like this required a lot of preplanning for me. This wasn't long after my surgery and hospital stay at Gillette, so I thought of all my needs for a formal dinner and a sitting schedule that stretched out over many hours. But thankfully, this wedding didn't have a dance. Angie was there, too, so we both felt the hours in my chair were not overdoing it.

Dinner was over. Doug seemed to be fitting in with everyone. A wonderful evening was coming to a close. Yet, suddenly, I was in the middle of my least favorite wedding tradition: the dreaded bouquet toss!

There are many reasons to hate the bouquet toss. First, it draws attention to the fact that I am single. Oh, it's fun when you are twelve with single status. It might even be okay for the high school girl because, if she catches the bouquet, it implies that she has the potential to get married. It's inevitable. She might be too young at the moment, but she's marriage-ready once she's old enough.

For the chronically single woman, this flower-throwing tradition is a reminder to her, and every person in the room, that if she catches the flowers, she also needs to catch the man, sooner rather than later. The clock is ticking. She has a responsibility to grab her guy and schedule the next big event. Maybe I'm overstating this, but I can tell you that, by thirty years old, this part of the wedding reception had lost its charm.

Then there was reason number two, a big factor for my hatred of the flower-tossing tradition: I can't catch.

Every time I rolled into the crowd to be a good sport, to participate in this single woman's ceremonial rite, I prepared for a possible smack in the face. I could already feel it. I grimaced with anticipation.

Think about it—I can't reach out and grab the wad of flora as it flies within reach. I can put up my hands to block it, like a front-row volleyball player back in my playing days, but I feel silly looking like I'm afraid of flowers.

I can extend much further than any doctor ever predicted with my limited upper-arm movement. But my reaction time is really slow. Most of the time, thankfully, the bouquet flew in the opposite direction of me. A sigh of relief would follow. However, I recall a few times when flowers brushed past my face in a near miss.

At Vernessa's event, I was paying close attention to the pace of the wedding activities, hoping I could time an exit just prior to bouquet-throwing. I was deliberately easing toward the door of an adjoining room, where food and drink and cordial conversation were the focus. I remember telling Doug, "Hey, let's head into the other room. I'd love a cupcake . . ."

We were having the best time! Doug made it look so easy meeting friends and David and Vernessa's families. This all seemed a joy to him, not a burden at all. Some guys dread being hauled to a wedding where they know absolutely no one on the guest list. My plan to dodge the attention and comments that come with bouquet-tossing seemed to be working. But just as I was motoring toward the doorway, Doug and I both heard a chorus of, "Tasha, get over here! She's throwing the bouquet! Vernessa's throwing the bouquet! You've gotta catch it this time. You're next! Right, Doug?"—wink, wink—"She has to catch this one. She's next!"

Oh, great. With a fake smile and encouragement from Doug himself—"Yep! She'd better get out there. Go on, Tash. For all the single ladies, right?"—I rolled to the center of one row of girls. There must have been about six or seven of us, hoping Vernessa's throwing arm was worn out from her long day as bride.

"Say, will you watch for me?" I asked the girl standing next to me in the small throng of young women. "If the flowers come flying this way, can you make sure they don't hit me in the face?" This was my typical request, and it usually worked.

No luck. Vernessa found me. She wound up and threw those flowers as far as she could. They smacked me in the face just as the crowd cheered, "Hey, Tasha! It's you! You're next!"

Once the sting wore off, I got swept away in the laughter, too.

And where was Doug? He waltzed in from the other room, apparently not afraid of the prospect which followed my so-called bouquet catch. While friends were saying, "You're next, you're next," Doug smiled, approached me with a kiss, and said, "Hey, I hear you caught the bouquet?!" We were definitely "meant for each other"—or so the wedding gossip claimed.

Okay, that one was well worth the swat in the face.

Vernessa threw the bouquet, and I got whacked in the face.

A LITTLE LATER IN THE SUMMER, Doug and I set out on a dream date, the Joyful Noise music festival. This was June, and we had our tickets for a full day of Christian music. Since Doug's forecast predicted a true summer day, my van was stocked with all the provisions needed for a long stretch away from home. The Honda would double as my respite facility, too, when I needed a break from the sun and humidity.

I love heat! Doug learned this in our early months of winter dating. My poor circulation, due to inactivity, guarantees that summer will always be my favorite season. Yet this event would teach me a lifelong lesson: heat stroke can happen to anyone, even someone with limited body movement whose internal temp runs a couple of degrees lower than normal. I re-member Darcy Pohland telling me that the older she got, the harder it was for her to handle the heat. I flashed back to my friend's words as I was experiencing this.

I tried pushing fluids, but it didn't seem to matter. As bands rotated to and from stage, the relentless sun beat down upon us. A musician Doug recognized, Matt Maher, would perform soon. All the signs showed I should be in the air-conditioned van! But my mind argued. *I can't leave now—not when we are having such a good time. What kind of girlfriend does that?* Yet, as the day progressed, I sensed I was losing it. I was having difficulty answering questions and forming words when someone tried to talk to me. *I have to cover. Doug can't know this. I'll take a break when Mandisa is done performing.*

"Isn't this great?" someone in the crowd asked. "Who's your favorite?"

"I . . . the . . . a . . ." Wow. My mouth formed the words, but nothing came out! I was like a babbling baby who had to learn language all over again.

So, with an hour left before Matt Maher would take the stage, I finally surrendered and told Doug, "I need a break in the van."

"You want me to come with you?" he offered.

"Oh, no—no worries. I don't want you to miss such good music." Actually, there's no way I said all of this; I just thought it. I couldn't get any more than "Nope, you stay" out of my mouth, and I turned to motor back to the parking spot.

I recall texting Angie: "Pray for me. It is 90 degrees out, and I don't know how much longer I can sit in this heat."

She texted back immediately.

"I'm praying for you," Angie replied. She was watching Isabel's volleyball game and figured I would take the right precautions.

I'm so worn out. There's just no shade out there. The sun is beating down on me!

I recall seeing a sliver of shade by the concession stand. When Doug and I moseyed up to order some food, I maneuvered my chair so that the skinny line of shade beamed over me. But it hardly made a temperature difference.

Tell Doug! He'll understand. This is risky! I knew I had underplayed the whole situation for Doug. I began bargaining with myself to be more honest with him.

And ruin his good time? No way. I was so afraid the extra precautions would take the spontaneity away.

He is having such a good time—I can tell. He won't want to date someone who can't hang out like a normal person for an event like this.

Lots of people are sensitive to sun, Tasha. It's not that unusual. I tried again to use my voice of reason.

This half of my inner battle made sense, but I was afraid, afraid of being honest with Doug. Afraid he'd see me as a big hassle and killjoy for the day.

Would he rather have to call an ambulance for you?

Well. I'm drinking lots of water. Feeling much better now!

It was true. With the air conditioner of the van blowing directly on me for almost an hour, I felt ready to go back to our spot in the crowd.

Promise yourself: If you start to lose it again, you'll tell Doug.

Okay, okay, I will. I promise! But I'm gonna go back. The van door opened. *Doug's gonna wonder if I left.*

I could hear the music again. As I motored back to our spot in the crowd, I noticed Doug talking with someone new.

Hmmm . . . who is she?

As I wheeled through the heat to join Doug again, I felt the nausea and dizziness coming back. But one look at this attractive young woman—apparently enjoying the music as well—and I felt a surge of consciousness. A kind of divine energy suddenly hit me. I was not about to turn around and head back to the van.

I smiled as I rolled up and took my spot next to Doug, and I semi-listened as he introduced me to the goddess standing next to him.

Of course she had to be beautiful. Long dark brown hair, all tan and thin, with perfect skin. She kept leaning into Doug, to sing along, or ask him questions about his favorite band.

Yikes! I was jealous. But this had nothing to do with Doug. He was just being his usual friendly self, meeting and talking with people around him.

He always did this. Why would I be surprised or bothered by this? Maybe because of the heat; maybe because events like this remind me that I'm different, that I stand out in a crowd of strangers. I began to hear the most ridiculous thoughts, which I could not "stuff."

There were so many beautiful women there. They all seemed fun and happy. They could stand, right by Doug's side. They could drink a gallon of water and then walk to the bathroom whenever they needed to go.

I don't have a chance.

By the end of my first book, I stated in a confident voice that I was "strong enough to wait" for the right one. I wasn't lying. I shared what I truly believed, that I have so much to bring to a relationship. And I did! I was quite aware of the gifts I could bring, whether it was for work, a friendship, or a romance. When I'm all in, I'm all in! Yet despite this confidence, and despite all of the signs that Doug was attracted to and committed to pursuing a relationship with me, I fought a quiet undercurrent of doubts.

In a word, I was insecure. Regardless of how happy a woman might be in the early stages of a relationship, the little insecurities of dating take her mind hostage. And I don't think it is just me. I think most women experience this. And perhaps men do, too. But I think my gender takes the prize for overanalyzing the things we view as flaws. So as we spend more time together, we are facing the fear that the man will find out the truth and that he will be turned off by it. The ego boost that comes with the attention from a new man gradually fades as self-worth anxieties invade our confidence. Most of us have something that makes us feel we have reason to be insecure, as if we would be worthy if all of our individual flaws were fixed. Sadly, this causes us to settle in relationships and even stay in unhealthy situations.

- I'm too tall.
- I'm too short.
- I need to lose weight.
- I have three kids at home; he won't be interested in dating my family.
- When he realizes the debt that I have, he'll drop me for sure.
- When he finds out I have (insert health issue), he'll be gone.

Brené Brown says this best in her book, *The Gifts of Imperfection: Let Go of Who You Think You're Supposed to Be and Embrace Who You Are*. Her words jumped off the page in one passage, as if she read my mind. How can we consider this artificial condition of the "worthiness of being loved"? I now know that we are all worthy to be loved, right where we are, or as Brené Brown puts it, " . . . worthy now. Not if. Not when. We are worthy of love and belonging now. Right this minute. As is."

I have fought my list of insecurities:

- I can't run to greet him with a surprise hug.
- I can't slow dance with him . . . well, not in the traditional way.
- We can't stroll hand-in-hand down a park path.
- As he pulls into the driveway, I can't spontaneously jump into the front seat of his car.
- I can't cook him a nice dinner.
- I need to have a personal care worker with me for overnight events.

I knew Doug was the right guy for me. He has helped me see the advantages to this list:

- I can do all of the driving. This is a modern date where the woman picks up the man.
- We quickly found some favorite places—repeated visits to buildings with accessibility (e.g., Caribou Coffee).
- At music festivals, the designated seating for wheelchairs is like VIP treatment.
- Romantic evenings at home with a movie on Amazon Prime help us avoid crowds and overpriced popcorn.
- We can stroll hand-in-hand down any paved path, and thanks to the ADA, almost every city has one through its park, often riverside, with very romantic views.

Doug is the one who often reminds me that dates by definition are superficial. You dress up, you're on your best behavior, you are in a good mood. You put on a show that life is great! This has its place in the world. It provides a break from reality, and everyone should do it. But hospital stays and daily cares reveal the truth. Early on, when I apologized for some arduous task that quadriplegia requires, he leaned over and whispered to me, "This is life. This is reality. This is how people bond. And I want to know everything about you."

Our conversation got pretty personal that night. In fact, Doug and I finally had the conversation of how I go to the bathroom. I explained my bowel care program and how I empty my bladder using a catheter. He admitted that he wondered if there was a small hole in the floor of the van.

"A hole in my van? What?" I asked Doug to explain.

"Well, you always go back to the van to pee. I just thought . . . did you have something rigged up, maybe there was a spot for the cath tubing to drain, every time we backed up, I expected to see a puddle, but then there wasn't one . . ."

Lesson learned in why I needed to tell Doug everything at that point. We definitely laugh about this now.

Many years ago, God spared my life after an accident that left me in a wheelchair. And I had to find someone who had the potential to understand why I love my life. I get to travel; I share my life; I feel rewarded when audiences get perspective from hearing my story, remembering their lives are valuable, too. I thank God every day that life took this turn. And now I have taken another turn. I have found someone else to share this with—someone who sees that my situation isn't tragic. It's amazing!

CHAPTER SEVEN

OHIO OR BUST

"I WANT TO GO ALONG."

My skin had completely healed and I was back to my normal long schedule of sitting in my chair. My manuscript's final draft was nearly ready for the publisher. And Doug announced, "I'm gonna cancel my plans to go out West this summer. I'd like to spend my vacation time with you. I want to go to Ohio."

"Really? Are you sure? I'll be tied up with the pageant. I'm pretty locked into their agenda the whole week . . ."

"Yeah, I know how events like this can go; they have your days pre-planned. But I still want to go."

Let's back up a few months. As Doug and I were getting to know one another, he mentioned that his tentative summer vacation plan was to go West to visit his aunt and uncle. He would return to his old stomping grounds in Colorado to spend time with Aunt Christine and Uncle Rod, wonderful people who had opened their home to Doug when he was a college student. They were his pseudo-parents while Doug pursued his second bachelor's degree—the one that gave him the skills to succeed as a meteorologist.

While Doug lived with Rod and Chris for four years, his uncle's experience in the Navy taught him some discipline that Doug hadn't experienced during his first round of college at Michigan. Doug earned a bachelor's in history without needing too many rules from his own mom and dad. Life in Colorado would be different.

With Uncle Rod's expectations that Doug keep things efficient, clean, and organized, Doug's time-management improved. He realized he could not only balance school and work, but he could also maintain good grades while working two, sometimes three, jobs.

His work experience in Colorado started with restaurant jobs. But then a desk job in communications came up—something more related to his resume. When that project was done and the job ended, Doug found himself temporarily at Starbucks until an NCAR position (the National Center for Atmospheric Research) in Boulder—as well as an entry-level TV job in Cheyenne—became available. After working three different jobs in his last year of school, he was excited to accept one permanent, full-time meteorology position in Eau Claire, Wisconsin. Here was his chance to move back to the Midwest.

Although Doug says he sometimes behaved like a typical college man, clashing with the grown-ups and their high expectations, he ended his time in Colorado with gratitude and love for all Chris and Rod had done for him. He vowed he would visit frequently after the move to Eau Claire, and at first it seemed easy. But once he had the chief meteorology job at WQOW, he found it even harder to get away.

By the time I met Doug, it had been five years since his last visit. He was feeling the urge to see his Colorado friends and visit the couple who had given him not only a room in their home, but also some great parental guidance at a time when he needed it. Now, when he humbly reminisces about those years, he sounds genuinely grateful for the additional guidance of his uncle. Doug told me a story of how Uncle Rod definitely played the role of a strict dad when his nephew made the rash decision to lease a new car that was beyond his means, just to impress some girl he met.

Apparently, Doug received a flyer in the mail tempting him to trade in his '89 Dodge Shadow for a shiny, candy apple–red convertible.

Doug called his aunt, who immediately said, "Turn around and walk out of there right now. Your car runs just fine. Do not get hooked into buying something you will regret."

Doug stayed. After the lease was signed and Doug had placed the down payment on his credit card, he decided to drive over and surprise the girl he was seeing.

"What happened?" I asked.

"The girl broke up with me," Doug said. "I had double the other car payments. My aunt told me maybe I could get out of it . . . something about a forty-eight-hour waiting period."

"Did it work?" I asked.

"Nah. I was stuck with the lease for two years."

"Well, I'm glad that girl broke up with you," I said with a smile.

I understood why a visit to his aunt and uncle's, as well as a potential concert while there, sounded like a good trip. Yet, as the year progressed, and we spent every possible weekend together, Doug shifted his interest to Ohio. I was shocked but felt closer than ever to this man who would spend his precious vacation time crammed in a crowded van.

Destination: beauty pageant!

"I know it'll be a crowded van ride, but you're gonna win this contest, and I can't imagine not being there."

He seemed so sure that I would win Ms. Wheelchair USA. I loved his confidence in me. But an undertow of doubts and fears that Doug would have access to my twenty-four-seven routine crept in at the thought of him joining our Ohio trip plans. The same concerns I had while guarding my daily cares at the hospital came rushing back in full focus. I was guarded, but I knew deep down that if he truly loved me, he would have to know everything about me.

The pageant was a media event; I would need to give my all that week. I knew I didn't have to entertain Doug. I never worried that he would be bored or put off that I was tied up with the pageant itinerary. Maybe it was his history degree. Maybe it was his interest in music and travel. Whatever the reasons, Doug was, and is, an independent man whose own experiences have taught him to find intrigue in any city. If I had to be whisked away to a photo session or a pageant practice, Doug would find something to do. But, I wondered, how would I guard my privacy when I was already sharing close quarters with an entourage of supporters?

The day before departure, Rachel stopped in for some prepageant massage therapy. When I voiced my insecurities about Doug coming along on the trip, she was the first to call out, "Where's that book! Sounds like you need a shot of Beth Moore. I hear insecurity creeping in . . ." Rachel started rummaging through my office book shelves for effect, and it worked. Enough said.

"I know, you're right. He wants to come along for a reason," I acknowledged.

"Yep. He loves you, Tasha. You are going to be making the best memories on this trip! I can't wait to see you win!" Rachel's therapy skills clearly involved more than massage!

My van seating chart now included Doug.

Mom would do most of the driving. In 2012, she was still one of my most valued team members regarding travel. The van's driver's seat could be placed to allow for a nondisabled driver, but at the time of the pageant, Mom was one of the only people who had the understanding and technical skills to take on the van's sensitive steering system. A huge fan of travel, she could endure just about any road trip. And I had to count on her, since arm pain impaired my ability to drive much of that trip. Caused by an adjustment in my wheelchair's backrest, something was digging into my armpit when in driving position. We simply didn't have time for an appointment to fix this. Hence, Mom would be at the helm for much of this trip.

I wore a TLSO—Thoracic Lumbar Sacral Orthosis, or a turtle shell— for ten years to help me sit up straight after I was diagnosed with scoliosis. Although this support was fairly comfortable for those healing years right after the accident, I found it quite cumbersome over time. And, frankly, a turtle shell is not exactly a good wardrobe choice when dating. Another good thing that resulted from my boyfriend just prior to meeting Doug was his push to pursue a replacement for the TLSO. The thing was hot, restrictive, and I had to wear bigger clothes over it. Thus, before meeting Doug, I had switched to an SSO . . . the same brace, but now part of my chair's backrest.

Mom was a vital member of this trip for many reasons. My organized mother could do anything a caregiver could do—well, except my hair. One of my ongoing jokes with Mom is that, despite her many talents, hairstyle work is not one of them. Teenagers often get annoyed with their own long, thick hair. Imagine my frustration in not being able to pull mine back, or even brush it with my own hands. Mom tried. She persevered, but I have left the hairstyling to a caregiver for years.

Now, visualize this: we were packed for our early morning trek to Eau Claire to pick up Doug and to meet his mom for the first time. The Honda front end included me in my chair, plus Mom in the passenger seat. The back area was occupied by my caregiver, with room for Doug to climb over the mounds of food, water, costume changes, and multiple suitcases for all those spending the week in Ohio. The van had one seat left for Melissa, my college friend who would join my entourage on our stop near Chicago. Doug's mom must have wondered what kind of vacation her son would have with a van full of women and all their stuff!

I drove for the first four hours, but Mom took the wheel when my arm pain became unbearable. I moved my chair to the middle of the van, Melissa moved to the passenger seat, and Doug, trapped in by coolers and luggage, kept my caregiver company in the back bench area.

"Nobody drink anything. It's too much work to climb out for the bathroom!" I'm not sure if this was announced, but it was a consensus by everyone in the van.

Thirteen hours later, after minimal stops, we entered our hotel and checked into a suite designed to sleep eight. Doug claimed the couch in the living room. Melissa and Mom took one room, and I split the second room with my caregiver.

We soon discovered the bedroom doors didn't close and lock properly, so I was constantly on the watch for Doug, reminding my caregiver to secure the door the best way she could. I didn't want Doug to see everything.

Having him a door away from my private cares was close enough to my disabled world. Mom and Melissa understood and helped protect my privacy while I kept a ridiculously hectic schedule of interviews, pageant rehearsals, social events, and photo sessions. Doug would either show his commitment after the hectic week or find an excuse to be long gone.

Yes, Beth Moore's voice came to me more than once that week. Most of the time I listened to her wisdom because Doug handled this girls' world like a pro. And in hindsight, I believe this trip finally led me to a place of peace about it, about all my insecurities. I loved Doug, and knew that with love comes trust. If he were to leave after this trip, I would survive. The pageant gave me the opportunity to apply Beth Moore's principles and ideas, which meant that if Doug chose a different path—one without me in the picture—I would be okay with it. I had to trust in God's plan, which took most of the worry away.

Plus, Doug acted like he had no regrets for trading in his trip out West for the pageant adventure. At times, he excused himself and went off to read and relax by the pool. But when the itinerary allowed family members and friends, Doug wanted to be there for the social events. Since he had a career in media, he seemed knowledgeable and curious about the television and livestreaming aspect of the pageant. He genuinely enjoyed all this prep for the show.

He met the pageant hosts and many of the business partners and sponsors. And he met my competition—the beautiful young women vying for the title. Every contestant, representing her home state, was disabled in some way, but often with fewer limitations than me. I observed gorgeous girls with their eyes on Doug, most of them outgoing and charming when he stopped to chat or ask how things were going.

What would Beth Moore say, what would Beth Moore say . . .

Doug makes friends wherever he goes, but my insecurity reared its jealous eyes at times. I understand his friendly, relaxed banter with people now, but during pageant week, it made me insecure and reserved at times. I did my best to camouflage this, but one of the contestants told me later, once we had formed a friendship, "You were kind of intimidating."

"What?" I laughed.

If she only knew how worried I was! Not only was I amazed by the beauty and talent of all the other pageant contestants, I also feared my boyfriend was opening his eyes to the fact that maybe Tasha Schuh was not so special after all.

My first book narrates the actual pageant, play-by-play. The events on and off stage, the excitement, seeing Doug and so many of my family members there! Angie, Scott, and the girls drove to Ohio, on their way back from a summer trip to Niagara Falls. And Rachel flew in to cheer me on! I loved the drama of waiting as I was passed up for a number of preliminary honors, only to hear the final announcement—"and Ms. Wheelchair USA for 2012 is . . . Tasha Schuh!"

Thinking back, I often wonder about the little things that made Doug and me grow closer that week, even in a packed crowd, during a whirlwind of prearranged activities. One of my favorite events on the Ms. Wheelchair USA agenda probably explains why I was never in the running for Miss Congeniality. When I saw this listed on the contestant calendar, it made me question out loud, "Who plans a swing dance party for a bunch of girls in wheelchairs?"

This was perhaps a tactless thing to say—except it was true.

"Let me see that." Doug must have thought I was kidding or reading it wrong.

"I'm not making this up. It says right here: a swing dance party, the night before the televised pageant." One of the other girls had informed me earlier with as much bewilderment as Doug seemed to voice now. We double-checked our itineraries and asked a few more contestants who verified that this wasn't a misprint.

More irony hit us when I reminded Doug, "And one of the first things you had listed on your ChristianMingle profile was that you hate to dance."

True story: Doug's profile included a statement, "Doesn't like dancing." This was a bonus for me! Dancing was something I endured from time to time, at weddings, swirling around in my chair with a phony smile plastered on my face. Doug and I had talked about this early on. We both agreed, we always wondered what something so awkward looked like. How can a person relax and let loose when all they can imagine is that they dance like Elaine from *Seinfeld?*

We arrived at a local school. Apparently the son of one staffer attended the school and got permission to use some gym space. But even the hired instructor looked befuddled when all these lovely ladies rolled in and lined up for lessons.

"Oh, boy," Doug stated quietly through his teeth. "I don't think that dance teacher was expecting this."

I complied, wheeled up along the others, kept my thoughts to myself, and waited to hear what some of the girls thought of this social hour. I wasn't the only one who found this event strange.

"What the . . . ? Are you kidding me?" were just a few of the comments said by the other pageant contestants.

The instructor, cordial and obviously a good dancer, suggested some moves and even had some ideas for modifications. The music energized the room, without much else happening.

"Okay," Doug said suddenly, initiating the first move. "We can do this. Let's just have fun," he whispered in my ear as he grabbed my hand.

I shot him a confused look, but I certainly didn't want to be a negative Nelly. "Just have fun," Doug said again, a little louder this time.

Oh, my. He's going to do this. And I am going to have to follow his lead.

So, yes, we got the party started, and suddenly there were others twirling in their chairs, laughing and going along with as much of the dance movement as they could rally. Doug and I laughed and moved in our own unique ways, and were grateful this was not part of the televised portion of the official pageant the next night.

Once again, I learned that attitude is everything. We had a blast that night! I was so thankful for Doug, who helped me knock down more walls. His attitude of "don't worry; who cares," showed me that even after all of these years of practice, after ignoring thousands of funny looks, after hours of sharing my life with an audience, after confronting hundreds of personal questions, I still had lessons to learn. Lessons that only swing dancing in a wheelchair can teach, lessons that trusting someone you love will complete. The cool thing was that event was just a warm-up for Doug, who would compete just two months later as his TV station's representative in the Eau Claire version of *Dancing with the Stars*.

Doug and I swing dancing.

Returning to Ms. Wheelchair USA the next year brought a whole new experience. This was my summer to give up the crown—to pass it to the head of Ashlee Lundvall, Ms. Wyoming, a beautiful, talented, athletic woman with many accomplishments.

Ashlee has become my very dear friend and has truly calmed so many of my fears about love, marriage, and intimacy. Although she is two years younger than me, I listened to her like a big sister with all the experience. I might have been crowning her that summer, but she was the one already married with a little girl, Addison. By that second pageant experience, we realized how much we had in common.

She, too, had her accident at sixteen years old. We were both over six feet tall, and although Ashlee was a paraplegic, the details of her fall—in her case, from a hay rack—seemed to mirror mine. I will always be indebted to her candidness, although I recognized that some of our spinal injury differences meant I was just going to have to find out what married life would be like on my own.

Another Ashley, Ms. Florida from the first year of the pageant, married a man who is also in a wheelchair. Both of these women prove over and over again that the world of disabilities is often an open book. And quite frankly, meeting and connecting on so many topics related to living with a disability proved to be the greatest gains of my pageant experiences. Until Ms. Wheelchair USA, most people I had met who depended on a wheelchair for mobility were men! In my first book, I talk about the small percentage of paraplegics and quadriplegics who are female. The pageant world opened my network to young women with a similar lifestyle. Ashlee and Ashley allowed me to question them about love, marriage, having children, and even things as personal as sex on your wedding night.

This handsome, nondisabled husband of mine would handle the interesting realities and sudden fears of Tasha Schuh. Having Doug along on the pageant trip challenged my inhibitions yet helped me believe him when he sometimes whispered in my ear, "Tasha Schuh, I'm gonna marry you someday."

CHAPTER EIGHT

A COLD PROPOSAL

AFTER DOUG SPENT THE warmth of July in Ohio, he leveraged for an autumn break in Grand Marais, Minnesota. This was a favorite fall retreat for Doug; he tried to book a few nights there every year. Apparently he discovered it shortly after his arrival in Eau Claire back in 2002, tucked along the frigid North Shore of Lake Superior. Early in the fall season he would take a ride up north—way up north, to the often chilly shoreline of this scenic, remote town.

"I want you to come with me this year," he said.

"In October? North of Highway 8? After Labor Day? I don't know . . . sounds cold."

"Come on. You'll love it. The drive is spectacular! And when the sun shines off the water, it really warms up during the daytime."

Everyone knows Lake Superior is the deepest and coldest of the Great Lakes. I know people who won't swim in it even in the summer. The water never truly warms up. Famous ships have gone down in those icy depths, and songs have lamented the men who all died. Thank you, Gordon Lightfoot, for leaving this indelible fear of Lake Superior in my mind forever with the somber melody of "The Wreck of the *Edmund Fitzgerald*."

Doug made a reservation for Aspen Lodge. The Holiday Inn, his usual choice, was already booked. How could I say no? Doug wanted me to experience all of the things he loved. He wanted me to share in God's natural beauty, the very place that helped him bounce back when life took its occasional dive.

When I reflect on his persistent pleas to check my calendar, I get it now. "I need to know your schedule. I want to plan this trip." I heard that line so many times that summer. This was surprising from a laid-back guy who didn't usually make definite plans more than a couple of weeks in advance.

But I understood why this was different. We needed extra space for a caregiver, plus a wheelchair-accessible room. I needed to have at least two nights free from speaking in order to make the drive worth it for us. Everything took longer with me in the picture. Doug had certainly learned this from the van ride to and from Ohio, as well as the summer music festival. I chalked it up to a boyfriend who really wanted to go up north, which meant he would do all of the legwork for this trip.

Still, I had my concerns with tagging along to a place that was not designed for a quadriplegic. I, Freeze Baby, would have to pack heavy sweaters, scarves to wrap my neck, and extra blankets.

"I don't know how long I will last outside, Doug." His love for the brisk air of early autumn in the Northwoods made me wonder, *Was this something we just wouldn't share? Would I disappoint him if we could only enjoy the fall colors from a North Shore drive in my toasty van?* A popular song often invaded my thoughts at times like this. "Safe," by Britt Nicole, seemed to narrate my insecurities. The lyrics described what it was like to be afraid to let someone in. For so long, I worked so hard at it. I repressed any desires to be with someone else. I protected my independence by exercising thoughts of what I wanted in life, no compromises. But one line from Britt Nicole's song got me every time: "Your love is worth the risk." Doug's energy and commitment to make this a special retreat for both of us made me flip my attitude. If this is what he wanted, I'd do my best to go along and enjoy it, no more worries.

No one has ever been more thankful for an attitude reversal than me! To say I didn't see this coming is an understatement. Even with subtle hints from Angie—"He wants to know your ring size, Tasha. He's going to ask you soon . . ."—I still didn't think Doug was ready for the biggest commitment of them all. This trip was another stepping stone toward the inevitable, maybe. I needed to garner another opportunity to share in something Doug loved—this special, cold place that he hoped we both would love.

Angie wasn't the only one who thought Doug might propose. Melissa was convinced that Doug intended to propose, but who knew when.

Block it outta your mind, Tasha. It won't happen yet. For one thing, he's super busy catching up at work since we got back from Ohio. He hasn't had time to plan anything since the pageant. He's too busy with dance practice.

Doug had emceed WQOW's *Dancing with the Eau Claire Stars* fundraiser the past several years. But this time, he agreed to be a contestant, which meant hours of practice.

I agreed with Melissa and Angie. We truly loved each other, thus I felt a proposal was imminent. But time was needed for Doug to think and plan. Plus, we hadn't even dated a year, although distance certainly does have a way of making people cut to the chase. Living and working in two different towns helped us appreciate the precious short weekends and gave us permission to talk about important things . . . deep things that couples might take years to get to. Doug and I were also at an age where we clearly knew what we wanted. We just hadn't experienced enough time together to visualize the whole plan. The sheer time it takes to envision popping the question, well, there weren't enough hours in the calendar at this point. Doug couldn't possibly be ready.

Our drive toward Grand Marais that sunny morning reminded us of God's gifts found in a changing world. We marveled at the peak fall colors but noticed fewer and fewer leaves as we made our way along Highway 61. Britt Nicole's song resonated in my head. I knew Doug's love was worth the risk. Worth a road trip toward a destination I would have never chosen on my own. I shed my fears and felt God's grace to appreciate a chilly but glorious place, mostly because Doug loved it. But also because we made amazing memories there.

Ecclesiastes 3 seemed to narrate the autumn vistas as the van hugged the rustic North Shore: "To everything there is a season, and a time to every purpose under Heaven." As I drove, I had a flash from the past—a quick vision of my accident. Not a day goes by without this happening,

The day before our engagement, we stopped at Gooseberry Falls, North Shore, Lake Superior.

although it's usually fleeting. I think of the accident, the fall, as my time to be born again, the birth of a New Tasha, after a mishap took so much.

That morning with Doug, I pondered for a moment . . . wondering if he would have preferred the Old Tasha Schuh. The Tasha who would have hiked and biked the North Shore, who would have taken a dive from the springboard if the hotel pool had one. Just as soon as that thought emerged, another took its place. This time, it was the thought that I probably wouldn't have met Doug if circumstances had been different. Because New Tasha was born, God blessed me with the time, the experience, and the patience to meet someone this wonderful. My tragedy, my gain.

The miles leading up to Grand Marais had me feeling like a kid at Christmas. Signs for Gooseberry Falls State Park and Split Rock Lighthouse reminded me that I loved surprises, and cruising the extra miles to park on the shoreline at Grand Marais was worth the wait. My mind drifted to my last conversation with Angie.

"He wants to get a ring; don't let him pick it out."

"But I love surprises." I was the kid who refused to sneak a peek even when Mom had poorly hidden Christmas presents at our house. Many of my friends told stories of finding bags in closets, and knowing exactly what was coming on Christmas morning. I would never snoop and take the chance of missing the magic that comes from an unexpected gift.

But Angie was basically telling me this was not a new Barbie, nor the difference between a pink or a yellow bike. "We are talking about a diamond setting, Tasha. One that you have to live with for the rest of your life. I think you want some say in this."

Well, there hasn't been time to pick out a ring. So get it out of your head. We've been too busy.

Suddenly the *Welcome to Grand Marais, Population 1,351* sign appeared on the quiet highway. The Aspen Lodge had our room ready for check-in.

"Two queen beds. Three adults. Yes, it's all set for you." The front desk clerk handed Doug a key.

Some people might find it odd that we shared a room, and that my caregiver stayed with us as well. Since we had made our pact to postpone intimacy before marriage—one of those deep discussions we tackled during our dating days and nights—why not at least be in the same room together? We still wanted to be as close as we could be every hour of the day. And since most of my caregivers are also close friends, there was never any question of this arrangement.

Doug had to agree to be out of the room when I was dealing with cares. But after Ohio, there was never any need to explain that he had to get ready for the day and out the door before me. He could get some coffee, plan our Lake Superior day, read a morning paper—exercising his independence while my cares were being completed. In fact, at this point in our relationship, neither of us envisioned that Doug would ever be a part of those cares. Little did I know how much he would eventually take on and how thankful I would be for his willingness to get involved. Yet, for now, he was my boyfriend. And a room for three was perfect for our Grand Marais weekend.

We settled in after dinner at a restaurant called Sven and Ole's. "I need a picture of that restaurant sign." I couldn't wait to show my rehab doctor, Dr. Christopherson, the physical medicine specialist who has been with me since my accident. A true Minnesotan, he was full of Sven and Ole jokes.

After so many miles, we all seemed to be tired. No plans to set an alarm— the longer I slept in, the warmer it would be! But Doug was up and out early the next morning. And he gave me a strong cue to follow his lead.

"It's going to rain later in the day," Doug said. "Let's get going a little earlier. There are some things you have to see before the weather turns." He clearly had an agenda.

It was cold—about forty degrees that morning. "Let's pull out the warmest sweater I own!" Wearing my heaviest sweater, with my lower half wrapped in a blanket, I overheard Doug asking a server for our hot chocolate to go.

"Let's head for the dock. It's an awesome morning. You have to see the shoreline before the clouds and rain roll in." Doug seemed really eager to get outside, but with the ominous sky, I totally understood. We would have plenty of time to sit in front of the hotel fireplace soon.

Our teeth were chattering, but I could see why Doug loved this view of the Lake Superior shoreline so much.

Suddenly, he put his drink cup down and pulled out a piece of paper.

"Tasha, I have something I want to read to you."

"What? You look so serious. What's going on?"

"Just listen." And Doug proceeded to read the sweetest, most unexpected poem, while I sat in shock and tried to listen to every word.

"'Falling Leaves,' by me," he smiled.

The leaves have changed, their colors dazzling the eye,
Days are getting shorter, the sun disappearing from the sky.
Pumpkins will be carved and children will go out,
and hopefully get lots of candy so as not to pout.

The taste of apple cider will fill the roof of my mouth,
and the Canadian geese will make their long journey south.
Round the corner comes a time to give thanks and praise,
for the homes that we have and the children that we raise.
The turkey will be carved and the potatoes will be dipped
in homemade gravy, while the topping for the pie is whipped.

And thereafter comes the time that all on Earth love,
a time to give thanks to our great Lord above.
This year I know exactly what I'll thank God for,
I'll thank him for this girl who makes my spirits soar.
He brought you into my life for a reason, I'm quite
and every day I know you, I want to find out more.
Your sweetness is so clear that I'm sure everyone can see
the Ms. Wheelchair crown you deserve, evident to them and me.
A thousand nice things to say and the most beautiful smile,
sometimes I seem lost; then I pick up the phone and dial.
I look at the falling leaves and water, happy that you are here,
to experience this beauty from God that I hold so dear.

Stars will display themselves in the sky tonight,
But none of them compare to your radiant light.
From our first date I've had this yearning inside,
the upwelling in my soul like a moonlit summer tide.
I dream we're on the beach moving across the sand
the only sound are the waves; the only feel is your hand.
The air is warm as the sun grows dim in the sky.
Daylight is ending, I never want to say goodbye.
My arms around you, your head against my chest,
your kiss on my lips, it's simply the best.
I will go to sleep tonight and you will be in my dream,
you are close enough to hold, or so it will seem.
All my life I've longed to feel the way I do now,
upon reflecting, I just step back and say "wow."

A feeling like this doesn't come around every day,
when I'm with you I'm floating on cloud nine in every way.
Looking at the fallen leaves I know this to be true,
only three little words can describe it: "I love you!"
So with water in the background as perfect as a setting could be,
just four words left to say: "Will you marry me?"

My jaw dropped when I heard his last four words. *What? What is happening? Is this real? Or am I back in the hotel, dreaming?*

A few seconds passed. My utter shock made me respond, "Oh my gosh, oh my gosh, oh my gosh."

Doug interrupted, "Well?" Waiting for my answer, I hoped he would pinch me to make sure I hadn't just imagined his poem! He had choked up while reading it, fighting tears, I could tell. And now, afraid of what might happen if I delayed my answer for too long, I finally realized, I'd better speak up!

"Are you being serious?" I still had to get a grip on this—a trip, a proposal, and a ring? Yes, he was holding a beautiful engagement ring. I vaguely remember him setting his poem down to reach into his pocket. *Can I push rewind? This is all happening so fast. It's surreal!*

I was convinced he had no time to plan this! But sure enough, here Doug was, down on one knee, waiting for my reply. "What's your answer, Tasha?"

"Yes, I'll marry you!" Lots of cheering, lots of kisses . . . and then, "Yes, yes, yes, yes, yes!"

Doug pulled out his phone. We needed to capture this. After some pretty toothy smiles, we would share the news with my caregiver. Doug had kissed off most of my lipstick in the first minute after saying "yes"! We were obnoxiously happy, despite the ring of lipstick around both of our mouths. The selfies captured the reality and chaotic emotion that came with this moment!

"Oh, my gosh, this ring is beautiful! When did you have time? How did you even know what to do?" I had a million questions, but Doug just wanted to say "I love you" a thousand times and tell me how excited he was that he had surprised me. After a few more photos, we were off to the warmth of the hotel lobby to take it all in.

"Yes! He proposed! Of course, I said yes!" This was a common phone conversation as I called Mom, Dad and his wife Dianne, Angie, Scott and the girls, Ryan, Nikki and the boys, Rachel, Melissa, and numerous others. The rest of the day, in fact, was spent reliving those moments leading up to the poem, the ring coming out of his pocket, and the vital question that would change our lives forever. If one of the locals even hinted at the slightest curiosity over my giddiness, I chimed in with, "As a matter of fact, we are celebrating! We just got engaged!"

Back at the hotel, showing off the ring.

Our servers at the restaurant that evening, the art gallery attendant, the hotel front desk clerk—they all received a close-up of my ring and more detail of the proposal than they probably wished to hear.

"Yes, a poem—by the shore—just this morning. No, I had no idea! Yep, he's amazing, alright. I love surprises."

The next day, all the way home, I thanked God for this wonderful man who blessed my life and would continue to do so for years to come.

"What do you think? Was this a good plan? Didn't I have you fooled? Ha, you were clueless, weren't you?"

Doug was gloating, and I couldn't have been more supportive.

"Yes, you got me. I was definitely surprised! I'm still in shock! I don't know how you did any of this. But I do know I'm lucky." So lucky, and grateful that God graced me with the good sense to love a surprise.

CHAPTER NINE

THE WEDDING PLANNERS

THE DRIVE HOME FROM Grand Marais was just as scenic as the drive north had been. But I hardly noticed since we had so much to discuss. I had a million questions! However, the wedding plans needed to move forward with little delay if we intended to get married in 2013.

We narrowed down a date pretty quickly since I knew I would not make a cold-weather bride. In Wisconsin, this meant August heat would accommodate me, which left less than a year to nail down the particulars for our very special event. I needed a wedding planner—someone who could orchestrate a whole lot of detail without stressing me out.

The first wedding planner to call into question was Doug himself.

"How in the world did you pull this off?"

"What?"

"This proposal?"

"Oh, I don't know. We've been talking about being together forever for a while now, and—"

"Yeah, but when in the world did you have time to plan? My parents knew! Angie and Ryan knew! You asked permission? The ring? The poem? I don't know how you pulled this off! And kept it a surprise!"

I wasn't trying to flatter Doug. I sincerely wanted to know how he accomplished all of this without my knowledge. Helping with some of the Ms. Wheelchair USA details that followed the pageant, getting back to work at Channel 18, volunteering to participate in a local charity version of *Dancing with the Stars,* and rehearsing for Karaoke for the Cure, another annual emcee responsibility, Doug spent every moment since July either working or driving to Ellsworth to see me.

"You had six weeks of dance rehearsals. How did you have time to shop for a ring? When did you talk with my parents?"

I found out that he had been plotting for months, but Doug agreed, his schedule was so tight, he had to ask Angie, Ryan, and my Mom for permission to propose right under my nose!

"Well, I asked all of them at your mom's house. I think it was Labor Day weekend. Yeah, the cookout at your mom's."

"And Dad?"

"Uhh, that came later—I think at that Bay City event." Doug was trying to remember all the details. I really wanted to know. It just meant so much that he went to all of this trouble to surprise me.

"What? I spoke at that event. How did I not hear you talking with Dad about this?"

"I don't know. I guess I just waited until someone else was talking to you. Someone always wants a word with Tasha Schuh. I waited until you were focused on someone else, and then I slipped into a little conversation with your dad."

"Sneaky!" I was giving him a hard time, but deep down, I felt such love and joy for the elaborate conspiracy Doug had going on behind my back. Suddenly the phone rang and I had Angie, my next wedding planner, on Bluetooth in the van.

"August—this year?" Angie was usually the confident one. We were sisters switching roles for once. "Are you sure? Well, I don't know. That's so soon. Do you want me to check the church calendar? I can tell you already, I know there's a wedding on the second Saturday of that month."

"Yes, check it, please, and get back to us. That will help so much."

Within minutes, Angie called back.

"Okay, here's what you have to work around. Tyler Nelson is getting married on August 3."

Tyler was an old family friend. Our moms were neighbors and best girl-friends all through school, and then both got married and had children about the same time. Hard to believe that Tyler and I got along like siblings a dozen years ago, playing games at their family cabin near Hayward, Wisconsin, and retrieving golf balls while our moms shot eighteen holes at Telemark Country Club. How fitting that, all these years later, we were getting married in the same month.

"The church"—Abundant Life in River Falls—"is booked for August 10, as well as the last part of the month. August 17 . . . that's it. That's what's open. Unless you take a Friday. But I'm telling you, August 17 is the only Saturday you have available."

"That'll work!" Both Doug and I concurred as we continued down Highway 53 toward Eau Claire. Doug's charity events—things that came with the territory of being a TV broadcaster—had filled his calendar. But one thing we were certain of as we booked the church with Angie that day: Doug would be free all next August, since he was already planning to decline his contract with WQOW. I flashed back to the day when we discussed a career change for him and suddenly felt relief knowing his contract was up before our wedding month.

Some weeks earlier, Doug's decision to change jobs was in the works. "So what would this look like, if I got on board with your career and left the weather profession?"

Even before the word marriage was used, Doug and I had confronted the fact that the distance between Eau Claire and Ellsworth was too much. One of us would eventually have to move. And since my home had been custom-built for my situation, it was only logical that Doug would move to Ellsworth. He had decided to leave his job, and since he would soon be on the calendar to negotiate a new contract, he knew approximately when his departure would be: August 2—just two weeks before what now looked like our wedding date.

Doug had accompanied me on a number of speaking engagements. He learned pretty quickly the ins and outs of my role as an inspirational speaker. He knew I relied on a marketing assistant—an administrative secretary who fulfilled so many business tasks for me—and wondered which duties already matched well with his own career skills.

When I asked him if he truly could see himself working with me, he considered it. "Well, first, tell me exactly what you need done. What does this look like, if I leave my job to assist you? What could or would I do?"

That's easy to rattle off—all of the duties impeded by my disability, all of the things I find a struggle to do but are inherent in this line of work. I crossed my fingers and hoped my honesty wouldn't steer him away.

"Well, for starters, there's the paperwork," I said.

"Yeah, but what paperwork? Can you be specific?"

"Okay, but understand that on any given day, these things might be top priorities, or they might not come up at all. It's just the nature of owning and running your own business. Don't chicken out before I share them all, okay?" Like sticker shock when shopping for a new car, this list might overwhelm even the most seasoned marketing assistant:

- All spreadsheets; negotiating contracts for speaking engagements
- Keeping my engagement calendar: avoiding conflicts and filling gaps
- The bookings and transportation details to make them happen
- Emailing pictures, my bio, and any other requested info for all events
- Creating and signing contracts and sending them in a timely manner
- Mailing any advance items (e.g., shipping books now that my final draft was set to go)
- Book signing events: arranging, promoting, scheduling appearances related to the book's release
- Taking phone calls when I am unavailable
- All of our bookkeeping for our tax records, including my caregivers, our business, and our income and property
- Anything else I needed done, due to my lack of dexterity

I stopped for a moment, thinking, *I should really write this job description down.*

Pat, my marketing assistant, had taken my speaking business to a whole new level. She helped me organize; she added spreadsheets and calendars to confirm our events. These pieces eventually landed in Doug's charge. Thanks to Pat, Doug could ease into these duties, rather than have them all dropped in his lap right after the wedding.

Juanelle Teague, a speaking coach who at one time worked for Zig Zigler, introduced me to Pat, and I would be forever thankful. Joe Schmit, the sports director from KSTP Channel 5—an ABC affiliate in the Twin Cities—was someone who advised us on so many aspects of the speaking business. Also a professional presenter, Joe opened doors for us with tremendous opportunities that grew our speaking business. Clearly, Doug would benefit from all of these people, whether he met them directly or simply acquired their nuances for our business model.

"Isn't Pat your assistant who helps you from Texas?" Doug asked.

"Yep, she's done everything electronically for me," I clarified. "I have never met her in person. Isn't that incredible?"

"That's modern business for you," Doug replied.

"Anyway, she's ready to share some of her workload, so you can start learning anytime," I explained.

In fact, Pat would continue to do some things for me even after Doug and I were married. But once he made the transition, Doug would acquire all of Pat's responsibilities. Other people in the industry helped train Doug, as well. Over time, he learned all of the tasks these guiding professionals believed he needed to know in order to manage my career.

That day in the van, traveling home to plan our wedding and start a new life together, Doug was secure in the fact that he had a new career on the horizon.

CHAPTER TEN

GOD SITS FIRMLY ON HIS THRONE

I F WE TOOK INVENTORY of all that had to be done in less than a year for this big fat Wisconsin wedding to happen, we would have freaked out. Actually, freak-out moments occurred here and there, but Doug and I had such faith after the "big things" fell into place that an August wedding was just meant to be.

So, instead, I watched *My Big Fat Greek Wedding* on DVD more than once that year, just as a reminder that if a complicated family like Toula's could pull it off, we sure could.

Angie questioned our timeline once again, just for good measure.

"Are you sure you are firm with August? I don't want to rain on your parade, Tasha, but this might be pushing it. People plan eighteen months or two years out. Should we check a later date at the church?"

A winter wedding was out. And neither Doug nor I wanted to wait until the following summer.

"You know you have the pageant again. That's—what, maybe a month before your wedding date? You'll be in Ohio, crowning the next pageant winner." Angie was pretty close, even without a calendar in front of her.

"Three weeks," I replied.

"What?"

"Three weeks. The pageant is three weeks before our date."

"Tasha, that's cutting it close . . ."

"I know, but do you really think God fell off His throne, or what?"

My sister knew this reference right away. Some years back, we had both heard the same speaker talk about the fact that we worrywarts had to put all decisions in God's hands, that God sits firmly on His throne. In other words, quit trying to muscle your way through decisions. If it's a part of God's plan, things will work. Be diligent, trusting, and accepting when things take a turn, but do not worry. We both love this message and do our best to have faith that a strong power has our backs.

"Yes, Tasha. God has a plan for you, I know."

"So why would we question this? Why would the trip to Grand Marais have been so perfect? Why would Doug have found the most amazing ring for me? Why would there be one Saturday left, strategically placed on the August calendar for our church? If—" I was almost done with my point when Angie interrupted.

"If, what?"

"If God hadn't meant for us to plan and persevere! God did not fall off the throne when Doug and I got engaged. If this is what He wants, He already has everything figured out." I had her. Angie was smiling now.

And as always, she intended to make it all happen for me. "Okay, Tasha. Let's start calling. Just be aware, this isn't going to be easy. We have one or two dinner and reception choices from what I see, and that's it."

"God never said it would be easy. But He didn't fall off the throne, so . . ."

"So . . ."

"Let's look at the list."

"Okay, this is what I know."

She rattled off the information regarding a few local establishments large enough to accommodate a big wedding dinner and party.

"This one is taken, this one only has a small room available . . . you might have to go back to the idea of a Friday wedding, Tasha."

Cross off, cross off, cross off . . . the list of reception options was whittled down quickly. I realized that the best place would be the River Falls Golf Course. The back patio had a beautiful view.

Angie agreed and planned to call there the next day. We scheduled a tour for the weekend so that Doug could join us, and by the following Monday, River Falls Golf Course was booked.

"It's really the only place with availability capable of feeding two hundred and fifty people." I explained to Doug the morning of the tour.

"Five hundred, Tasha. You're up to about five hundred on your guest list." Mom and Angie reminded me that we needed a Plan B if the wedding ceremony included five hundred guests. Somehow, with a little creativity, we devised a plan to host two receptions: one at the church—a dessert reception for those who patiently waited in our receiving line. And one at the golf course—a traditional sit-down, catered meal, with DJ and music to follow.

"People will understand, Tasha," Angie and others explained. "The church has seats for seven hundred. Everyone who truly wants to witness your wedding can come. But feeding a full, formal dinner to five hundred guests just isn't feasible in western Wisconsin."

"I know, you're right. People will understand." But I was struggling with it.

"They're just so happy for you, Tasha. Like everyone from church—they've known you so long. They want to hear your vows, but they will understand that space is limited." So, with Mom and Angie's help, we started to design two different wedding invitations, two different desserts, and one ginormous list—although, at some point, I still felt the need to draw the line.

"Ugh! It's so hard!" I stated, not long after promising I would stop adding to the guest list. In fact, later, someone came up with the idea to stream the ceremony. All my friends who were so supportive over the years but could not attend the ceremony could watch on their computers. People like my relatives in Alabama, Doug's relatives in Oregon and Colorado, Ashlee and her husband, classmates who had moved away, many of my Facebook followers, and medical staff from Rochester. I feel so fortunate that a few of my closest nurses and therapists came to the wedding and reception. Yet, when Doug and I learned later that about five hundred additional people saw the ceremony streamed online, we were so grateful we had said yes when this option was offered.

With the big calendar items secured—church and reception venue—the celebration could begin. With a full roster of attendants and ushers, readers, and musicians, the party planning was on, starting with dress shopping.

Well, if God hadn't fallen off the throne over a ten-month planning period, I had to trust that He would be there for my biggest challenge—finding the dress! I required a wedding gown that would flow elegantly from a motorized wheelchair, something I could sit in for twelve to sixteen hours. I set out on a mission to outfit myself and the wedding party, starting at David's Bridal.

My five attendants seemed to solve the dress test pretty easily. Melissa lived the furthest away, so shopping at a reliable, national chain meant she could pick her dress up on her terms. Once it was ordered, any alterations could be accomplished near her home in Illinois; she would be eight months pregnant for the ceremony. All of the others had the convenience of David's Bridal in nearby Woodbury. Angie, Melissa, and my dear friends Mary, Brooke, and Holly agreed on the colors—teal and dark purple—and the style with zero debate.

I wanted Vernessa and Rachel to be bridesmaids also, but there were not enough groomsmen. Doug never imagined a large wedding party, so this was already beyond his expectations. Therefore, I asked Vernessa and Rachel to serve as personal attendants and purchase dresses the same color as the bridesmaids. In my mind, they were indeed my bridesmaids.

With a little initiative and help from those involved, all wedding plans thus far had fallen into place, as if God had predestined every detail. With loving, cooperative friends like this, finding my dress would be just another joyful step in the adventure, right? Why, then, did this task seem such a challenge? I had the design in my mind, elegant all around. However, I would not be the traditional bride, gliding down the aisle, trailing a long, lacy train or a tiered, ruffled back. Although this narrowed my choices significantly, I vowed to keep Bridezilla at bay.

Bridal gowns—my very first experience in a changing room since my accident. As much as I love new clothes, I have developed a keen eye for size. I usually buy it, take it home, try it on, then deal with returns if I don't like the fit. If only I could skip the changing room drill this time. Yet something so important and so costly posed many different requirements for a long day of looking good. Suddenly, a sales woman began handing me size 6 dresses. Feeling awkward, I remembered why I ordered clothes online and tried them at home.

I wanted to cry. Not a single dress fit me.

The sales clerk assumed my small shoulders meant I was a petite size. "But a size 6 won't work. Things have to be very loose around my hips . . ." I wasn't worried about cath cares, as some readers might wonder. The size issue had more to do with the fact that I had been sitting in a wheelchair for sixteen years by this point. Gravity and a loss of muscle tone kidnapped my legs and transformed them. My hips had changed, as predicted by some of the hospital staff. They had warned me that I would have to accept a new look—a flat butt. Gone were the tight quads and glutes of a volleyball player. Over time, my physical therapist's prediction came true. And on this day, nothing seemed to fit! Alterations were common for most brides, but the situation overwhelmed me and made me feel as if I had no business in this shop.

Ruffles, tight waistlines, beads that cut into my skin like razors—suddenly every dress had a personality of its own, determined to sabotage my day.

Angie was the first to notice that I wanted to cry. Finally, one dress looked as if it might work. I didn't love it, but oh, well. I was ready to settle if it meant I could quit trying to stuff it . . . if I could quit trying to pretend that everything was fine.

The bridal shop had a tradition—if you found "the one," ring the bell. The sales staff will make an announcement, and all in the shopping party will cheer for the bride!

I was ready to ring the bell. I found something that would work, it would suffice. But then, my sister stopped me.

"Go ahead, tell them to ring the bell. This is fine," I reassured Angie.

"Nope. I don't think you want to do this."

"What? Angie, just ring the bell. It's just a dress, and this will work. I can get it on and off, it's white . . ." I took inventory of why I didn't hate this dress.

"But you don't love it," Angie replied as we debated in the dressing room. "You deserve to have a gown that you love. That's every bride's right."

"Nah, I'm not an 'I love it' girl. You know that. We're talking clothes. Not Doug. This is not a big deal. If it fits and it's easy to get on and off, that's what matters."

"Sorry," Angie persisted. "I'm not letting you buy this until I hear you say 'I love it!'"

So Angie wrote down the order number and told the sales staff we might be back.

Angie was right.

On the very next trip—this time to a bridal shop in Stillwater, Minnesota—we found it: the perfect dress! Something I knew intuitively was meant for me and that Doug would love too. I rolled into the shop on a miserably cold winter day in January, wheeled around one corner, and there it was—hanging on display! Sleeveless, with delicate pearl beading from top to bottom; strapless so that I could wear a single necklace of pearls and earrings which went with the embellished torso; and the skirt not layered or too full, so it would drape down and over my legs which were set at a ninety-degree angle for the entire day. Doug would wear a classic black tuxedo, an elegant off-white shirt and tie to match my light cream–colored dress, and a pocket kerchief and small white calla lily to accent it all and to match the calla lilies and succulents mixed in my own bouquet. Those trumpet-shaped flowers added so much!

"I'm sorry, Mom and Melissa. This is so hard to get on," I said as beads of sweat dripped down both of their faces. They were working so hard to get this dress on me. Realizing that my seat cushion created an extra obstacle, we just couldn't get the full effect to tell if we liked the skirt. Mom knew this dress would be easier to try on at my house. So she asked a woman working, "Is there any way you would let us take this dress home?"

"Well, we don't normally do that. But under the circumstances, yes. If you give me your credit card information, I'll give you twenty-four hours to take it home and try it on there," replied the clerk, who turned out to be the owner. With the drive to and from Wisconsin, this was still a short window of time. But we were thankful for the deal. And the store owner at Stillwater's Raffiné Bridal Shop definitely went out on a limb for us, overlooking store policy.

The next morning, all curious, available women gathered at my home. It was a breakfast bridal club: Melissa, Angie, Mom, and my nieces, and we rang the imaginary bell at my house! It was unanimous. This was the perfect dress for me!

In the end, the company added fourteen inches of fabric to the design of my custom-made dress in order to extend the skirt to fully cover my long legs, which define much of my six-foot-two stature. I did not want my feet showing. Essentially, the dress company redesigned the entire dress for me by also taking the train off the back and really fitting it to my measurements. And they did all of this for free, an amazing gesture by both the owner of the bridal store and the company that made the dress. I felt this woman pulled some strings by understanding my story and wanting to accommodate my unique situation. I was so extremely grateful for the bridal shop's support.

"Mom," I said while we pulled the dress on one more time before returning to the Stillwater shop to finalize the purchase. "I love this dress."

"I can see why," Mom replied. "You look so beautiful! Let's get it back to Stillwater and make it official!"

CHAPTER ELEVEN

EAT, DRINK, AND BE MARRIED!

AUGUST 17 WAS QUICKLY approaching, so many friends and family members stepped forward to help us with the precelebration events. We were blessed with showers and parties and festivities that made the calendar pages fly off the wall. The hours of a year could not tick away any faster! Doug enjoyed the engagement party we had in November, about a month after our Grand Marais proposal trip. Some of my friends were just meeting Doug for the first time, and we certainly wanted a chance to blend as friends before our wedding hit the event calendar for everyone.

My mom's friends, my aunts, my church members, and my closest girl-friends all wanted to host showers. Registering at Target, Kohl's, and Bed Bath & Beyond was an early requirement, since the first shower took place in May. By the time my bridesmaids planned my last shower for late June, hosted at Brooke's house, we had agreed to extend things into the eve-ning—my bachelorette party.

Now, I wasn't much for wheeling around the Twin Cities to drink and show off as the bride-to-be. In fact, the spectacle of a bachelorette party turned me off completely. Yet I certainly wanted to celebrate this mon-umental occasion with women who had supported me along the way, through the ups and downs of single life, and who knew what a struggle it had been for me to find my independence. This bachelorette group witnessed me discovering a wonderful man who would support me in the life that I had started for myself. I love my friends, so there was much to celebrate!

Thus, the plan evolved that we girls would pack up the fabulous gifts received at Brooke's shower and head to Minneapolis for an evening of laughter and bonding at ComedySportz—an improv theater. A caravan of cars hit the highway toward Uptown where we laughed until we cried, ate some late-night appetizers, and reveled in the fact that the big day was planned and (hopefully) ready to go.

Stevie, one of my dearest friends—there when I stepped backward, there when I was comatose, there in rehab, and brave enough to ride with Grandma to Rochester for long visits on late school nights—was arguably a candidate for maid of honor! However, I asked Stevie to be an usher.

"I'll be a bridesmaid, if that's what you want," I recall him saying. And he would have done it! But I was already over quota with bridesmaids. We decided to put Stevie in a suit.

It wasn't difficult to talk him into joining the girls in Uptown.

"Hey, I want you to crash my bachelorette party in the Cities," I told him on the phone. And in Stevie fashion, he was not at all bothered by the fact that he would spend the entire night as the only man amongst a bunch of women.

After college, when most of my friends were busy with serious relationships and many were getting married, Stevie was not only one of my closest friends—he was my man-fix. Although never romantically involved, we so enjoyed each other's company. And I believe Stevie would agree. We both needed that opposite-gender relationship. Like a scene from *My Best Friend's Wedding*, we had established an agreement: if neither of us was married by age twenty-eight, we would tie the knot . . . with each other! Was it during *Grease* or *The Wizard of Oz*? I'm not sure during which show, but I recall sitting at the Sheldon Theatre having that conversation.

Oh, we've had our disagreements, which is likely why we didn't fall for each other. Our differences—how we see the world—are too pronounced. But I always felt loved by Stevie. And he knows I love him back, and will forever. Never has anyone felt so much support from one friend after such a catastrophe. He had to be a part of my wedding, and I hope he always knows how much this mattered to me.

I THINK THE PREWEDDING SUMMER event that may have caused the most talk was Doug's bachelor party, which was scheduled for Las Vegas—ten days before our wedding.

"And you're okay with this?" one friend asked me.

"Actually, I am. They'll be harmless." And I meant it. I truly trusted Doug and his friends.

This was a road trip for Doug, two of the groomsmen, and two other old friends. Plus, it served as a job-change celebration for Doug as he was leaving meteorology. WQOW had already hosted a wonderful farewell for him the previous weekend. The following Saturday, just hours after he gave his final televised weather forecast in Eau Claire, Doug hit the road for Las Vegas in one of his best man's vehicles. His good friend Dan owned Chippewa Valley Airport Shuttle Service. He could spare a van for the trip. I didn't know this at the time, but the guys set out for Vegas in Dan's shuttle van with an odometer reading of 665,000 miles!

As a few more people questioned my calm demeanor over Doug's road trip to Las Vegas—Sin City, the gambling mecca of the Western world—images of Doug and his buddies repeating scenes from *The Hangover* never really popped into my head. For one thing, I had not seen the movie. In addition, Doug and four other men had only five days to traverse 1,289 miles—which included stops at historic Wall Drug and Deadwood South Dakota, a full day at Yellowstone National Park, and pit stops for eating and sleeping—before turning around and hightailing it back to Wisconsin. Who had time to get into trouble?

"Hi, honey. I miss you so much!" Doug would call every day. "Oh, the guys are out gambling. You know me, I have a hard time spending money on fast food, much less wasting it on a slot machine. It was 104 degrees this afternoon, so I was by the pool working on my prewedding tan!"

We spent most of our talk-time counting down to our wedding. "Just think, in twelve days and five hours I'll be walking down the aisle with you."

This countdown was a spin-off of Doug's original countdown started in our dating days of long-distance waiting. From the time he left my driveway, Doug would have the countdown on. "Okay," he would say, looking at his watch. "In just 120 hours, I'll be driving into Ellsworth to see you again."

I loved the sentiment, but it sounded too long! So, I made him stop—no, actually, delay—the countdown until a few days into the week.

"My new rule: you can't start the countdown out loud until Wednesday."

He complied, so on Wednesday evenings I would hear something like, "Just think, honey, in 62 hours, I'll be making the turn into your driveway . . ."

Doug's new countdown was specifically for the wedding. Days and hours and minutes were ticking off. I think he started the whole thing about six months out. He's such a numbers guy! And I'm now a believer in the old adage: opposites attract!

Maybe I'm too trusting. But I don't think so. The cross-country drive gave Doug a mission—a goal to spend quality time with his friends.

Plus, by this time, I had learned from Beth Moore and through confidential talks with my sister that controlling someone is never healthy. Yes, I had my times of worry and fear, but at the end of the day, I realized that trying to control Doug's every move for fear that he might be lying to me was a waste of time.

Angie said it best when she shared her faith in her own husband, "If he doesn't want to be with me, it's his loss . . . I don't want to be with someone who doesn't want to be with me." Her words were very healing, as they reminded me that I could only control myself—and by trying to control Doug, I would only be pushing him away. If he rejected me, oh well. I had to believe that someone else would come into my life who would love and commit to me.

But on the eve of Doug's departure for Vegas, it was clear for both of us: being married soon was the true reward, regardless of all of these prenuptial festivities. Engagement parties, bridal showers, and road trips were all wonderful traditions. Some of these events brought family, attendants, and witnesses together. With such varied backgrounds, we used this time as a chance to bond toward the big day—to meet and mix our friends and families, since we truly were becoming one. But if anyone considers these things a bride or groom's "last hoorah"—a last chance to misbehave before making a commitment—well, that person doesn't sound ready for lifelong vows.

So Doug went to Vegas, I monitored the wedding's final details, and we prepared for the main event.

The Bachelor Party continues in Las Vegas, NV.

ONCE BACK HOME IN WISCONSIN, my personal meteorologist proclaimed his five-day forecast with a level of optimism that seemed Godsent. "It's looking good—partly sunny, low eighties. A few clouds for relief when we go outdoors for pictures. I think we're going to like this," Doug shared, just days before the wedding.

People often ask if I was nervous. I don't think that's the right word for it. Doug and I spent plenty of time planning what we hoped would be a meaningful ceremony—for us as well as all of our guests. So tweaking it and adjusting the order of things while trying to maintain just the right length kept us both attentive. This may be what added some sleepless nights to that last week. But I wouldn't call it "nerves." We just wanted everything to be so meaningful for our guests and for ourselves.

It was Tuesday evening or Wednesday morning, the week of the wedding, when he called me to say, "Only ninety-six hours to go, honey, and then you're Mrs. Drogorub for life!"

I had full intention of taking on Doug's last name after the wedding. Our marriage license reads Tasha Schuh-Drogorub, since Doug's legal family name is Drogorub. Some careful readers might recall that Drogorub is the name I used to introduce Doug as my new boyfriend at the end of *My Last Step Backward*. Hard as we tried, in our first speaking engagements after the wedding, announcing me as a keynote speaker definitely lost some pizzazz as event hosts inevitably stumbled over Doug's last name. We gave in. Doug went back to his TV name, Doug Michaels—Michael is his middle name—and I returned to my business name of Tasha Schuh.

Of course, my legal last name is still Schuh-Drogorub. We just use Schuh and Michaels professionally. It's so much easier; however, I still have fun spelling out the formal name when calling for appointments!

Random receptionist: "What is your last name?"
Me: "Schuh-Drogorub."
Random receptionist: "Excuse me?"
Me: "Schuh-Drogorub."
Random (annoyed) receptionist: "Can you please spell that?"

Yes, it's my name, but I still have the anxiety of a National Spelling Bee participant when I have to rattle it off out loud!

MOM HOSTED, AND AUNT SHIRLEY and Uncle Gordy hired a caterer to provide a traditional full BBQ dinner for our Rehearsal Thursday. Although Doug's mom had shared her concern that our marriage meant her only son would spend less and less time with his parents, this dinner seemed to be the opportunity to reassure her of quite the opposite. My repeated words, "You are not losing a son . . . you're gaining a daughter and her whole big family!" became reality to Rachelle and Dale that evening. What a joyful night!

"See you in thirty-two hours and twenty-three minutes," Doug said as we kissed goodnight. We talked on the phone as often as we could that week.

"We're having our nails done now, some of the bridal party." I explained to Doug how some of us enjoyed having manicures done the morning before the ceremony—whoever was available, since some couldn't get off work. It was a busy time for everyone. I recall Dad went to Men's Wearhouse for his tux.

And oh, yes—Doug got new brakes.

Really? The shop—on the day before the wedding? Yes, it's true. Wouldn't you know it—brakes, rotors and all. There couldn't be worse timing for a big auto-repair bill. Sometimes you just can't predict these things. His car had to be fixed, and since Doug's goal was not to see me until I strolled down the aisle on Saturday, why not take care of it then—the day before the wedding!

"Only twenty-five hours and seven minutes till showtime." Doug had plenty of time to count down and call me as he waited in the mechanic's lounge area.

The final evening before the wedding, Doug called to say, "In just twelve hours, you'll be coming down that aisle, ready to become my wife."

I continued to plan for my long day in this full and frilly dress. The usual cares still had to be scheduled. The true sense of the personal attendant's role took full bloom as soon as the day started. I was so grateful that I had more than one to call upon. Rachel said she heard her name called nonstop all day long. She was exhausted by the end of the night.

I didn't actually "schedule" Rachel and Vernessa, but in hindsight, I should have. At one point, I had plans to ask a third person to be a personal attendant. I look back and realize how much I needed that third attendant. If I didn't keep these girls hopping, someone else did.

Therefore, Mom and Brooke jumped to my call frequently throughout the day. I'm sure Angie did, too, as she kept the junior attendants in place—at least through the grand march. My nieces and nephews marched down the aisle: Isabel first, followed by Anna and Cameron, then little Ella and Connor, in early elementary school at the time. Angie's and Ryan's attention needed to be with their children. And although I had all of my caregivers on the guest list, if I could do it again, I would have scheduled them to check in with me for cares throughout the day.

One girl was hired for the end of the night—her own hotel room included—so my bedtime cares were covered. In the morning, she was again scheduled to get me out of bed, dress me, and ready me for another full day.

Despite the responsibility to divvy out so many unique duties on a day I would experience only once in my life, things went as I had dreamed. Doug and I felt God's grace from the moment we woke up that morning, until we slumbered off in utter exhaustion at the end of it all.

Some weeks back, I had accepted the fact that, because of my physical limitations, I wouldn't experience the traditional ceremonial preparations, but we would come as close as possible. As I privately dressed at home with Mom and my caregiver, Maddison, I thanked God that all went smoothly.

"You look so beautiful," Mom said with tears in her eyes. "I'm so proud of you, Tasha. This is going to be a perfect day."

With my dress on, I drove myself to church for the rest of my preparations—hair, makeup, flowers.

Locking into my driver's seat, I thought, *This dress is so white! How am I going to get from here to church without getting full of grease or dirt?* I tried not to worry. To safeguard, I wore a cream flannel sheet over my dress as I covertly rolled into the children's church room at Abundant Life. This room served as my private apartment. The sheet continued to protect me as we played with makeup colors and sprayed my hair, hoping it would stay in style for hours.

My makeup would be done by a friend and former caregiver. She and Britney, another caregiver, were scheduled that morning to arrive at my church with back-to-back time slots. Britney, who was only thirteen when she started doing cares for me, had finished cosmetology school while working for me part-time. As my primary hair stylist, I still count on Britney, a true artist, to style my hair for everything. Looking back, I can't believe that in the planning stages, I actually considered going to a beauty shop on our wedding morning. At that time, Britney was so new at doing hair. But I knew her sincere desire to do the best job on a day that mattered so much to me. And the result was beautiful! She did a style that was so unique—one that did not even come to mind until that morning. Everyone loved it!

Britney's work of art.

With hair, makeup, and dress feeling comfortably complete, I turned around to face my bridal party and family. Would Doug approve? Would he think, "Wow, this was worth the wait"? That was my hope! And from everyone's reaction, I think they believed that Doug's jaw would drop—just as I wanted.

Doug was actually the one who was adamant about not seeing me for a full day before the ceremony. He hoped for that total surprise moment—and he got it! I made it unseen to the side room at church. I posed for pictures with everyone but Doug, and then waited patiently for my cue to join Mom and Dad in procession.

Moments before the procession, I waited patiently in a room at my church. Although I couldn't see them, I sensed the full crowd. All our guests would soon face Mom and Dad and me gliding down the aisle together.

With my wedding party leading the way, I waited just a bit longer before rolling slowly toward center stage. This was the church that changed my life. It was where Pastor Kevin and Pastor Ted inspired me and others to maintain a life through Christ. They had both played specific roles as I grew in my faith. I couldn't have asked just one of them to officiate the ceremony. So Doug and I agreed we should ask them both.

If my clock was right, Dad and Isabel were now singing their duet, "When God Made You." I could only imagine what this sounded like, since I remained in my prep room at this point.

Dad showed off his talent with an earlier tune he performed with his group, the Summer Time Quartet: "The Longest Time" in four-part harmony. Doug had rewritten the lyrics to fit our day. Although we are both Billy Joel fans, some of the original words didn't match the occasion of a wedding. We both agreed, "The song should really complement our vows!" So Doug took a chance that Billy Joel would not be offended. His revision was perfect—appropriate for our commitment to each other, "for the longest time."

The song was flawless! Dad and his fellow musicians sounded great!

Chorus: Oh, oh, oh
For the longest time
Oh, oh, oh
For the longest time

V. 1: When you said hello to me online
Your smile brought this certain song to mind
How else could I feel
This feeling seems so real
This hasn't happened for the longest time

V. 2: Once we thought to meet for our first date
But your nerves made you a little late
That's when I saw you
And I got the door for Tasha Schuh
I knew we'd be there for the longest time

Chorus

V. 3: On your deck I was weak in the knees
Thanks to all the annoying bees
I knew I loved you
And how you loved me too
We'd be together for the longest time

Bridge: I know this will last very long
You are so right
This is our song
Maybe we were meant to be
We've gone this far
And it's all that I've hoped for

V. 4: Only God knows how long we'll go on
I will love you till the day I'm gone
I'll pray for fifty years
Lots of laughs and few tears
We will be together for the longest time

Bridge: I had pleasant thoughts from the start
I said to myself
"Hold on to her heart"
She is clearly the woman meant for me
She's beautiful you see
And it's all that I hoped for

V. 5: I don't care what the world throws our way
I will always have these words to say
I want you so bad
And I think you ought to know that
I intend to hold you for the longest time

Chorus

Such a clever version of the song, and the harmony was pitch perfect! Although I remained in the back room at this point, my family told me later that Dad had no struggle with his voice, until he started his duet with Isabel.

I'm sure it was the emotion of the lyrics. He apparently teared up. And Isabel—wow, she got her chance to shine!

Isabel sang with more authority than I ever expected. What a sweet irony for her and for her grandpa; she had been the nervous one! Would I be able to razz Dad later about this? So who carried who through that song, Dad? Despite the pauses as he choked up a few times, Dad's emotion actually added to the meaning of the moment. It was truly a perfect start to the ceremony!

Feeling the love from so many people, incredible gifts came together that hour in church. I felt a calm come over me from the moment Mom and Dad guided me down the aisle toward Doug. Pastor Ted asked, "Who gives their permission for Tasha and Doug to marry?" They answered simultaneously, "We do."

Doug and I had anticipated an emotionally charged ceremony. One wedding we attended earlier that year was so moving that even the bride cried throughout the ceremony. We barely heard her vows since she was visibly and audibly sobbing through most of the service. We wondered, what could we do to stifle some of the emotion yet not diminish the meaning of the day? We needed some comic relief. Something that would complement the ceremony, not downgrade it.

Pastors Kevin and Ted often use a big screen to display a quick video clip demonstrating the power of their message at any given service. Doug loved these digital enhancements to the minister's message. We both did. And our ministers knew it, too.

Suddenly, just as the ceremonial welcome was about to begin, a clip from *The Princess Bride* filled the screen . . . the part where the highly decorated officiant at the wedding kicks off the ceremony with his garbled welcome of, "Marriage is what brings us together today."

Everyone loved it! Although my back was to our friends and family at this point, I heard the laughter break the anticipation, and I was so grateful that Pastor Ted's scene choice helped make our ceremony fun and different.

They did it again, soon after our reading about how important it is to "wear love." Ever hear of JibJab videos? A JibJab clip directly followed Pastor Ted's story of checking up on Doug soon after I met him. Yes, my "spiritual dad," as he refers to himself, who had made the call for a lunch date with Doug, loved and embraced Doug faster than I ever expected.

Pastor Ted warned me in advance of some big-screen surprises, but I truly did not know what would pop out at us. But I trusted Pastor Ted. I had been to a few weddings that seemed dry . . . not memorable. I so hoped that ours would be unique and unforgettable to everyone who attended. These spontaneous interruptions really did the trick!

So, just as the sermon ended, the big screen lit up—in animation this time! Cartoon Sonny and Cher broke into song with "I Got You Babe," and our faces filled the caricatures of the animated singers. A flash from the past, but everyone, young and old, knew this song!

The more traditional vows followed after a short time-out for our own pledges. Pastor Kevin helped us deliver our silly opening requests:

"Do you, Tasha, promise to watch two *Star Trek* movies or episodes per year with Doug?"

"Do you, Doug, promise to love Tasha whether she is covered in blanket, shawl, or scarf?"

"Do you, Tasha, promise to cheer for the Detroit Lions when they are not playing Green Bay Packers?"

"Do you, Doug, promise to watch three musicals per year with Tasha?" (Doug attempted to negotiate this item—"two?"—but failed.)

"Do you both vow to love each other, whether the temperature is seventy-two or eighty-two degrees?"

"We do!"

We were on to our next set of more traditional vows. It was time for the serious words we both privately planned and kept secret until this moment.

Doug started with his profession of vows:

"For the better part of my adult life, I searched in vain for a woman I could someday call my wife. It was when I gave my search over to God, however, that He introduced me to you. Our journey began with email conversations, progressed to hot chocolates at Caribou Coffee, and continues here today with our wedding. I knew love was developing for me the first night when I visited you at your house. As I was pulling away to go home, I noticed you sitting alone in front of your widow watching me go. All I wanted to do was run back inside and hug you. I prayed the day would come when I wouldn't have to leave anymore, and that day is today. As you know, I proposed to you through poetry, and so I thought what better way to pledge my love to you than with another poem."

Doug did it again! With hundreds of people listening, he shared his poem in a confident profession of his love for me. It was any woman's dream come true . . . beyond my own dream of how perfect this ceremony could be.

"I, Doug, take Tasha to be my wife,

to adore, cherish, and hold the rest of my life.

You will always be my companion, lover, and best friend

from this day forward until the very end.

If you are ever hurting and need a shoulder on which to cry

I will always provide mine without the need to ask why.

Finally, I promise to provide for and protect you.

All of this I declare before God with the words 'I do.'"

It was amazing. I didn't know if I had the endurance to follow through with my own vows after that! But I couldn't back down now. I had a grand plan for a "vow finale," which would require complete focus, courage, and divine intervention. All those years ago, after my accident, after my coma, after the doctors stated that I would not have the stomach muscles to sing, I now shock everyone, even myself, when I open my mouth, and without much strength to push it out . . . I sing. And that was my gift for Doug on our wedding day. For my final vow, I would break into song.

Please God, help me make this happen. Let me open my mouth and share my gift with Doug—for all to hear!

It was my turn for a profession of vows.

"I have been dreaming about this day since I was five years old while playing Barbies," I started to share. "The Prince that I would someday meet and spend the rest of my life with. But never would I imagine that he would be as wonderful as you. Never in my life have I known someone who has made me laugh like you do and melted my heart like you do."

I explained how I found something helpful as I composed my vows.

"I came across a list that I had written out in 2006. I titled this list 'What I Want in a Husband' and proceeded to write out all the things that I wanted God to include in the man that I would someday marry. I wrote this seven years ago, having never met you. But, as I read that list after completely forgetting about it for years, I just had to smile at how God heard my prayer and brought you into my life. To just list a few, I wrote:

- Loves God with all his heart, mind, and soul
- Loves to laugh
- Complements my personality—knows how to handle finances and is organized
- Caring, kind
- Loves to travel
- Wants kids
- Independent
- Loves me for who I am

I have prayed for you to come into my life and I see God's faithfulness as you fit everything in this list."

I noticed how quiet it was as I finished.

"The only thing that you didn't fit was that I wrote that you would be taller than me . . . but I think that was asking a little too much."

I paused as I heard people laugh.

"So knowing that God has brought us here today, I promise to love you unconditionally, to never take one moment for granted, and to respect you, cherish you, and adore you with all my heart every day of our lives together. I promise to work through difficult times, communicate about everything, and be there for you through life's ups and downs. Today I promise to be the right person"—I fought back tears—"that every day when I wake up I am concerned about your needs and how I can be the best wife to you. It is so hard to put into words all of my promises and so I will try to sum it up in this song."

I heard the music start. I focused on Doug's surprised face as I held the microphone steadily for my song. I had practiced for weeks after searching so long for the perfect song, something I had not performed as the "wedding singer" at someone else's event, something uniquely personal. I had considered composing my own special song, but there just wasn't time for that. This was definitely the song that spoke my heart, so once I altered a few things to make it truly ours—ironically, the real title is "Here We Stand"—I could commit to the idea that, for Doug, I could do this. I could serenade my husband in front of hundreds of guests. *When—God, make me strong!*

Here we are, face to face
Brought here together
By God's amazing grace
Into your eyes, I see myself
Living a life I've always dreamed about . . .
And as I am here before you
I can't help but adore you . . .
Here we are, in this moment now
I give my heart, I give my love
This is my vow
To you I swear, and I promise to
Give all I can, all I am I give to you
Here we are, hand in hand
United as one
By the promise of our love
I open my heart, and let you in
To live there forever as a lover and a friend
As I am here before you
I can't help but adore you . . .
Here we are, in this moment now
I give my heart, I give my love
This is my vow
To you I swear, and I promise to
Give all I can, all I am I give to you
Here we are, here we are
Here we are, In this moment now
I give my heart, I give my love
This is my vow
To you I swear, and I promise to
Give all I can, all I am I give to you
all I can, all I am, I give to you
Here we are, face to face

Brought here together
By God's amazing grace.

After a few other highlights, the ceremony ended and we prepared for
a receiving line that curled around and down the hallway. Both Doug and
I praised God over and over for the gift of this awesome day. We knew
that volunteers manned the dessert tables and punch bowls during that full
hour of hugs and pictures, although we never got a look at that part of the
planning! Friends congratulated us. Then our own photographer reunited
the wedding party and immediate family for photos in the church. After a
few personal cares in transition, Doug and I were in my van, making the
short drive to the golf course.

"Alright, who's been messing with the van?" I blurted out as we exited
church. "*Duck Dynasty?* Really?"

Yes, my brother-in-law, Scott, heard me announce more than once that
I did not want the traditional strings of beer cans dragging from the bride
and groom's lead car. He and Stevie's decorative camo theme definitely
got more attention in the parking lot and on the drive down Highway 35,
River Falls.

"Very funny, guys," I said as I locked into my side of the van to make
the drive across town. If they hadn't planned something, I would have
wondered what went wrong.

Our grand march introduced the entire wedding party as we entered the
reception room for dinner. I knew our first dance was coming after the
meal, so my nerves were a bit keyed up. But Doug and I had practiced at
my house about a week before the big day. Immediately after his Las Vegas
trip, Doug had found a spare evening. Imagine the two of us, conquering
the awkwardness of an able-bodied man leading a taller yet seated paralyzed partner in a dance. My gratitude flashed back to the Ms. Wheelchair
USA pageant, where Doug and I had made the best of the swing dance
event. If we could swing dance then, we could easily pull off one slow
dance.

Doug cooperated, but he questioned my need for a dance rehearsal.

"It's just one dance; we'll be fine."

Once again, Doug viewed another very public thing as "no big deal." He sees no stigma with a wife in a wheelchair. God has truly blessed me.

Deep down I think the source of my anxiety was not knowing Doug's side of the guest list very well. Our wedding day would be the first time I would meet some of his family and friends. My concern for their acceptance of Doug's decision to marry me, a quadriplegic, weighed heavy at times. I have learned, since then, I had nothing to worry about. Doug has experienced an outpouring of sincere support, from the time we were engaged until now, feeling it again and again with the celebration of each anniversary.

I guess I was afraid of looking awkward, yet deep down I knew that my insecurity about the whole thing was the greatest threat for awkwardness. This dance was tradition—expected. *Just go with the flow. Doug will make sure we're fine.*

"Let's do this," he whispered immediately after dinner.

Just like in our private rehearsal, Doug grasped my left hand and placed his right hand on my shoulder, while I operated the motion buttons of my chair to engage just enough swivel action to mimic a slow dance. Doug twirled around from time to time to add a little variety as everyone looked on.

Some guests later commented that watching us on the dance floor was the most touching part of the day. I realize now how close I was to saying, "We look so unnatural dancing, Doug. Let's just skip that part of the reception." I probably would have gotten my way. I'm so glad I didn't!

As we left the dance floor, Doug's parents caught our attention. They seemed to be enjoying the night as much as we had hoped.

With a smile, Doug's dad leaned toward me as we ended our first dance. "So, when do we get grandchildren?"

What? But we haven't even had our honeymoon yet, was my first reaction. Then his words hit me. I put my guard down. *Oh, wait. This is awesome . . . I'm really a part of this family.*

"Hey, now don't rush us," I joked back. I was definitely feeling welcomed into the family at this point.

Oddly, if I have one regret—and it is a small one—I wish I hadn't stayed out on the dance floor so long that night. Yes, after all my trepidation, after considering the option of no music and no dancing, I embraced the dancing with family and friends for what must have been hours! After Doug's dance with me, I returned for the next request, and I simply stayed out there! Before I noticed, it was quite late, and I hadn't even talked with a number of my guests.

I know, everyone tells me, this is okay . . . that guests were happy to see me happy. That's true, I am sure, but I do feel I missed out on the opportunity to visit and thank so many special people for taking time from their busy summer to be with us all night. To them, I want a redo, a chance to thank them personally.

The evening sped by. Exhausted, we pulled the duck decoys over to the hotel for our first special night together as husband and wife. My caregiver was waiting to help me out of the dreamlike dress that held up throughout the longest, most treasured day of my life.

Pastor Ted and Doug, tearing up as I come down the aisle.

Mom and Dad accompany me as I spy my prince at the front altar.

Pastor Kevin delivers our silly pledges as well as our more serious profession of vows.

My favorite picture from our wedding… the thrill of victory!

Doug's mom and dad, Rachelle and Dale.

My entire family—parents, siblings and their spouses, nieces, and nephews.

Our entire wedding party.

CHAPTER TWELVE

LOVE AND INTIMACY

DISCLAIMER: THIS CHAPTER IS rated PG-13, and parents should be warned that we are about to discuss mature content. Young readers, disabled or not, please read and discuss this with a trusted adult. Yes, this is the sex chapter, which may seem too blatant for some of our readers— but intimacy is a part of the human experience after marriage. We must acknowledge the fact that God created sex, and therefore we shouldn't shy away from it. On the contrary, we should pursue intimacy as an important part of a healthy, unselfish, loving experience. As a spinal cord injured (SCI) person, the act of sex is certainly different for me. But I hope to clarify why it is also better than if every nerve ending in my body still existed. And much of this has to do with the deep love and mutual respect I share with my husband.

I admit, I had all kinds of concerns about intimacy before—and after—meeting Doug. I truly did not know what an intimate relationship would be like after my accident. This was uncharted territory for me, and new to Doug as well. True, I had been sexually active before the accident; this is one of my biggest regrets. Doug's too. But now it was going to be different. I wondered—*Will I be disappointed? Will Doug be disappointed?* He knew what the experience with a nondisabled partner was like.

I don't want to embarrass my hubby too much, but all I can say is we have both been incredibly surprised and satisfied that our intimate relationship is far beyond anything we had experienced. Isn't it amazing what true love will bring?

Although I certainly don't have the credentials to hang a sign on my office door stating that I am a qualified sex therapist, I have learned a thing or two about the importance of closeness in a marriage. Plus, I am tired of reading books that claim to be the tell-all of a spinal cord injured life and then discover that they have, once again, skirted around some of the biggest challenges for those who live with paralysis. Therefore, Doug and I have agreed to share things openly . . . things about intimacy we learned in our first years of marriage.

I HAD A BEAUTIFUL WEDDING—a dream come true. Yet, the weight of one mystery—the wedding night—could not be ignored. True, the biggest justification for writing this chapter was that I was tired of the myths and misconceptions that plague people's thoughts regarding a couple's sex life when one partner happens to be disabled. However, after the wedding, I also had to face my own unknowns. Therefore, I hope to dispel the myths, which are often the result of modern movies—Hollywood's misrepresentations of disabled lovers. In the process, I hope to share some insights that will help any married couple pursue and nurture a healthy, trusting, active intimacy that will bring people closer than they ever thought possible.

Sex requires a special kind of communication, especially when one within the couple is disabled. Doug and I made a pact—a mature vow—that we would wait to experience intercourse until after our wedding. Oh, we shared a closeness on those weekends when Doug drove from Eau Claire to Ellsworth after a suspenseful countdown to our togetherness—"Just twenty-six hours before I turn in the driveway again!"—but living out our vow was not easy.

Doug slept in the guest room every time he stayed, to avoid the late-night drives back to Eau Claire and to guarantee we had optimum time together. We both knew from previous relationships that premarital sex had not guaranteed a successful bond. It just left us feeling empty and regretful once the relationship ended. So this time, waiting made the commitment more serious and more honorable. And we wanted to honor one another with the patience to wait until our commitment was genuine, lasting, and acceptable in God's sight. It just seemed right to say, "I don't need to have sex with you to know if I am truly in love and deeply and forever committed to you."

This being said, well before my wedding night, I battled some pre–Beth Moore insecurities. I truly wondered if Doug might find intimacy with me, at the very least, odd and awkward and, perhaps my greatest fear, unfulfilling. Yet faith, hope, love, and a little help from some loyal friends have a way of conquering fears.

Back up a few years to my "single" stretch, those miserable months before Doug. Mayo Clinic had asked me to appear in a video regarding sex, made by and for individuals with spinal cord injury.

"What? You want me in your film?!" I questioned one of my doctors. "Have you forgotten that I am not sexually active?"

My doctor explained that they wanted to interview me for their film to address many of the other factors regarding dating and being out and about as an active, social person.

"Many of the issues related to intimacy are different for young people in a wheelchair," he explained.

They hoped to reveal some insights from my busy lifestyle. In other words, I had some good habits in my pocket . . . habits that helped make a person attractive to others. For instance, I took the time to do my makeup and hair. And because I was out in public so much, my hygiene was a high priority. People who are in bed or homebound often let such things go. So, Mayo wanted to coach and encourage viewers to make the effort to be appealing to others.

The sex information would come later in the film. I was part of the preliminary work.

"Ah, I get it now. Sure. I can be in a sex video . . . as long as I don't have to talk about it or share anything about intercourse."

This must sound strange, I agree, but anything to further the cause for Mayo. And when the video was completed, I watched it, in all of its candidness. If the phrase "Shock and Awe" hadn't been copyright protected, I might have suggested it for Mayo's film title.

So, for me personally, here's the most jolting piece of information from the film: sometimes, some disabled people actually defecate during sex.

"What?! They poop?" I was appalled, and pretty sure I would remain inactive forever if this proved to be a common thing.

The first thing I do when I learn some new strange secret related to my disability is to ask the wheelchair world to validate it. My gratitude for medical staff who pursue the truth for their clients is endless. But theory must be supported by reality. Know your network. The first friend I asked was Holt.

He's my oldest and dearest friend with a disability, someone I initially visited at Courage Center. Our accidents were two months apart. You may recall Holt from my first book as the smart guy who told me to get over it and start using a tenodesis splint because I would gain incredible independence from this tool. How right he was!

I could ask Holt anything. I knew I had to have this conversation, and not surprisingly, he thought I was crazy.

"What? No! I don't poop when having intercourse. Come on."

"Well, what am I supposed to think? Mayo said it in their video."

"No, no. Never has happened." Then after a long pause, Holt added, "But maybe for girls it's different."

"What?!" I asked. Oh, my gosh! Where's Beth Moore? I was on my third round of her book by then. Just when you think you are a together, mature adult, a fear like this rears its ugliness.

I was freaked out, to say the least, so I returned to my faith in medicine and asked one of my doctors. He stated that the bladder is really the biggest concern.

"Tasha, you're worked up for no reason. You do your bowel care program on a regular basis to eliminate such worries."

This made sense. And by now, I had met friends, including Ashlee Lundvall, who could share with me the truth of their experiences without feeling it was TMI. I sent her an email saying that I had some questions about getting married, and she wrote back in such detail that I knew I had asked an expert and a sharing friend.

At the bottom of the email, after spilling many details of her and Russ's intimacy and sex life, she had a mini panic moment saying, "I hope this is what you were looking for. Because if you were expecting to talk about wedding registry stuff like china patterns, I probably overdid it."

"No! Your email was perfect! You knew exactly what I wanted to know!" I replied.

Ashlee was married by the time she competed in Ms. Wheelchair, and she confirmed: "Yes, the bladder could be a culprit. But we have to empty that anyway. Do what you normally do before any special activity."

But I was worried about logistics.

"Oh. Packaging," she said. "Yep. That's important."

"So, what if I want to wear lingerie?" I asked.

"Yeah. So. Wear one of those sexy negligees you got for a bridal shower gift. Doug will love it." Ashlee answered.

"But how do I plan for this?" I asked in frustration. "There's no spontaneity."

"Well, wait now. Think about it, Tasha." She was so patient with my worries. "Ask your caregiver to dress you. Then, Doug will come in and see he is in for a special night."

"But how do I get out of it?" I asked.

"Tasha. There isn't a husband alive who wouldn't like to unwrap his present."

I had a lot to learn.

In the years since this discussion, I have talked with some SCI individuals with similar concerns. A few seem to be experts. Some are even more naïve than me. When told to ask their doctors about it, some have said, "I don't even know what to ask."

Spinal cord injuries can do damage to sensation and motor function in the pelvic area. Some may not have any feeling in their genital region. Men can have difficulties getting and maintaining an erection. Women might lack vaginal lubrication because of their injury. We have all seen enough commercials to know that women can find medically safe lubricants to help, and men may use prescribed medicine to experience an erection. Some disabled men who've lost their ability for ejaculation have pursued implants and other options to extract sperm if having a child is part of their intimacy plan.

What I have learned in the advocacy circles is that most people can find excellent medical information from their physicians. Mayo Clinic is not the only health care system with helpful documentation regarding common problems like positioning. Although the message is usually "you have to invent it, you have to experiment" to find a way to enjoy sex after spinal cord injury, there certainly are stimulators and positioning aids, glider supports, pillows, and wedges to make intimate contact possible. Our bodies adapt. Many individuals with SCI share that intimacy may be different, which could be precisely why the emotional connection is so fulfilling.

BY THE TIME DOUG and I made our mini honeymoon trip, our "mini moon," to Door County, we entered our hotel with confidence that we had little to fear when it came to love and physical affection.

"Yes, we have a reservation for three: Mr. and Mrs. Doug Drogorub—I mean Michaels—Doug Michaels and Tasha Schuh, and caregiver . . ."

Doug handled our hotel reservation more fluently than this, but toggling back and forth from our professional to our legal names could be confusing. And there were three adults, not two, for a honeymoon weekend?

Despite our enthusiasm, we intuitively knew things were different as Doug unloaded the suitcase for our caregiver, and she crawled from the backseat after the long haul across the state of Wisconsin. We had made small talk along the way, but for miles my mind was reeling with questions. *Okay, with a caregiver along, how is this going to work?*

It's true. We couldn't be completely alone on trips like this. At least we weren't prepared to do so at that early stage of marriage. In our minds, we had to bring a third party along—and thought we always would.

Like a true honeymooning couple, we didn't leave the hotel much. Our caregiver enjoyed a lot of free time. She was just a phone call away if I

Doug's guns at work; swimming for the first time in years.

needed her. She did join us one evening for shopping as we made our way down Main Street. The Door County specialty shops had so much to offer—although one candy store turned out to be a terrible challenge since it was not accessible, and the clerk was annoyed by my needs. Beyond that, the area was charming and romantic—a perfect setting for an adventure in intimacy.

Now, I know that some of you flipped to this chapter before reading anything else, while some of you may never want to read this chapter at all. Others are probably predicting the very thing I had overheard at times that made me want to write candidly about this topic: "I don't think Tasha can have sex." Quite honestly, part of me wants to say, "That's none of your business!" And although Doug never heard any direct comments or questions about this, I have. So I will address the misconceptions directly.

This topic has become everybody's business since the world has been grossly misinformed by movies and media. In fact, myths exist because life for those dealing with a disability is still comfortably distant from most of society's experience. But let's agree on one thing right away: regardless of your values system, we live in a sexual society. And even when I feel unconditionally loved by my husband, I want to know that he is attracted to me and that his desires for a full married relationship can be fulfilled.

Nothing offends me more than hearing others question this aspect of my life.

One reason that I, rather than Doug, often hear the doubts and questions is that I welcome them. Within my public speaking engagements, I open all of my Q and A sessions by announcing that there isn't a topic regarding life as a quad that I won't confront. In other words, there isn't a question you can't ask.

"Ask me anything—I will answer if I honestly know, if it's part of my world."

This kind of invitation leads people to wonder about everything from going to the bathroom to having babies. So why wouldn't sex be a part of this curiosity? However, I am stunned more often by the assumptions, not the questions, that adults make regarding my personal intimacy. Here are a few that I have experienced:

1. Someone jumping into marriage with me is settling for less when it comes to sex and intimacy. Mayo Clinic's Patient Education video series seeks to dispel this very myth. Too many people believe that paralysis knocks out one's desires, that someone like me becomes an asexual individual, and therefore any partner would have to settle for life without sexual satisfaction. This couldn't be further from the truth. The desire still exists—and in most cases, the ability is also still there. As the video series states, "Part of the fun is figuring out what works."

I can't speak for everyone who has endured a spinal cord injury, but I can give you Mayo's findings that patients move on to sexual fulfillment and often discover intimacy that is heightened after they adjust from their injury. In my case, looking and feeling desirable has always been important to me. This aspect of my personality was not altered with my fall to the Sheldon Theater's concrete floor. Wanting Doug's attention is a priority in our relationship. And Doug will be the first to tell you that he never had to settle for less after we found each other.

Although we postponed intimacy for after the wedding, we both knew the desire was strong and my parts were still in place. Which leads me to . . .

2. I couldn't possibly get pregnant, so Doug must not want children. Again, the Mayo Clinic video series shares their extensive research on dating, sexuality, and even childbirth. Hence the title: *Feeling Your Way: Relationships and Sexuality After Spinal Cord Injury*. I strongly endorse this program, in which my opening remarks (taped before I met Doug) still ring true today. In the film, I talk about the fact that when I am out socially, maybe at a wedding, people sometimes find the courage to ask me, "So, Tasha, can you have kids?" I usually laugh out loud, which prompts them to wonder what I find so humorous. I have more than once replied, "You don't want to know if I can have kids; you want to know if I can have sex."

Again, Mayo used this clip in their sexuality video despite the fact that I was not sexually active when they filmed their research findings. They knew my experience was common. Curious minds want to know. Nondisabled people often doubt our capacity for sex, and I sometimes get the impression that they want their doubts validated.

In our early months of dating, Doug and I tackled the topic of having kids. We both love children and are thankful for nieces and nephews who give us a glimpse of the joy, as well as the work, that parenting brings. When I fell through the trapdoor many years ago, my reproductive organs did not fall out. I have the same possibility of getting pregnant as I had before my accident. I face concerns like monthly menstruation and birth control, like every woman in her childbearing years. In other words, please don't ever stereotype a physical disability as a sign of sterility. Doug and I said adamantly before our marriage that we would have children. This option still exists. Our desire to start a family is a recurring topic of discussion, which we will clarify later in this book.

3. This assumption is definitely related: An acquaintance once commented, "You can have children? Oh, I suppose there's artificial insemination these days. I mean, how would you get pregnant?"

"Excuse me," I answered. "But how would you get pregnant?" My candid reply seemed to take her by surprise. But seriously, to assume that I could not participate in the act of intercourse is a presumption that offends me.

And worse yet was when another person once stated frankly, "It's too bad you can't have sex. But, then again, you have a head and a mouth . . ."

I know I invite the most forward questions and comments by being so open about my life, but that one tops all. I set this woman straight by stating that my experience with intercourse could be as "traditional" as anyone's and left it at that.

Nevertheless, after confronting many of these comments, questions, and assumptions before the wedding, even Doug's reassuring love wasn't enough to calm my fears about sex after marriage. So I searched for more academic help on the matter. Mayo's DVD was a start, but I needed a second opinion. I recommend everyone—disabled or not—take time to search out what the experts have shared. A little Dr. Phil before nuptials is not a bad idea. I've heard this talk show host warn his viewers of the dangers of underpreparing for marriage. Dr. Phil has sharply pointed out that we devote more time and thought to the wedding day—one twenty-four-hour period in our lives—than we spend preparing for the obvious obstacles to a successful marriage. Another writer said we spend more time in driving lessons than we do in marriage preparation.

These candid observations reminded both Doug and I that we needed to acknowledge that intimacy should be studied and explored as an ongoing part of closeness in a relationship. Without turning this into a volume of Masters and Johnson, let me simply reference a few pearls of wisdom acquired during my "study" of marriage.

Lesson #1: Taking time to read some respected literature on love and sex has helped me on so many levels. Splitting time between information designed for those with SCI and information helpful for a broad, nondisabled audience has brought balance to my understanding of sex in a loving marriage.

I started with Sheila Wray Gregoire's book *The Good Girl's Guide to Great Sex (And You Thought Bad Girls Have All the Fun)*. This book allowed me to consider intimacy from a Christian woman's perspective, not a disabled person's point of view. Then, a number of online articles by Rachelle Friedman, who became a quadriplegic after a pool accident at her bachelorette party, helped me with the physical aspects of sex after paralysis. These thoughtful writers remind us that intimacy—falsely assumed to be a natural, spontaneous act of love—can actually become one of the most challenging, worrisome parts of every relationship. Surely it should bring nothing but joy and closeness to the couple involved. But as always, attitude is everything, and God's plan for our success in marriage does mean Doug and I need to be sensitive to each other's needs, communicate openly, and find time for closeness and intimacy, regardless of our busy lives. We must not take this aspect of our relationship for granted.

This brings me to Lesson #2: I had to stop focusing on others' ideas of what good sex was, including the media and entertainment industry's representations of intimacy. I firmly believe that women will not find fulfillment from competing with their girlfriends' talk of the big O. Nor will couples find intimacy at its closest level by trying to imitate Hollywood's version of sexiness.

This is where my friend Ashlee would lighten it up by saying, "I think you should make this a pop-up book, Tasha."

"I thought you planned to do that in your book," I usually shoot back at her.

Doug and I have learned that closeness is such an individual thing, especially if it involves a disability. And our uniqueness as a couple was what was key! I read somewhere that the O is not for orgasm, but for openness. Doug and I couldn't agree more. By being mutually open ourselves to the trust of authentic intimacy, nothing is more fulfilling, more comforting, or more exciting, all at the same time. The experience becomes our own big O, our own most intimate expression of love.

Yet I had to learn this through experience. Before my wedding, my mix of anticipation and fear led me to think back on questions many people had about my sexuality. I was asked more than once if I would experience orgasm. I vividly recall one woman going on about this, saying, "How awful for you." Then, in the next sentence, she admitted that she and her husband hadn't had sexual relations for years. And you're feeling bad for me? I was bothered by the fact that others were judging the medical likelihood that I wouldn't feel the big O, yet their own status of intimacy didn't sound worthy of envy. I was confused.

The summer before I was married, I thought so much about this. I talked again with my doctor, who said, "No, you won't have an orgasm in the way most women experience it. Things are in place, but paralyzed, after all."

Once married, I looked and listened for it. I became a student of the big O, wanting to prove my doctor wrong—like when I learned to sing without stomach muscles. I was a little bummed at first to accept that, rats, it was true. Tasha, no big O for you. But, funny, about the time I quit worrying about it, waiting for it in overfocused anticipation, something changed. I have discovered that making love with my husband is one big orgasm. I'm not expecting it, and suddenly everything is heightened. When I see Doug's pleasure, I experience something so awesome. What else could it be? I was a little disappointed at first, but when I began to abandon the expectation, things began to skyrocket. Pay attention to what's there. That's the fun part—you may suddenly experience something far more sensual and exciting than you ever imagined by trying so hard to find pleasure.

Doug and I got a king-sized bed right before the wedding—something soft for my skin but big enough for two people who slept alone for many years. Some people are surprised to learn that I don't need a special bed—that Doug and I picked out something that any couple could have. I couldn't wait to feel Doug pressed against me, to have his warm arms envelop me every evening. I hope any person with a disability realizes that although your sleep is important, some adjustment to sleeping with the one you love is so worth it. You will sleep better in the long run, because you have the joy which comes with closeness.

I've often shared that music is my favorite language in life. I catch myself singing out loud to Doug, "You make me feel like a natural woman." Some might remember the strong Carol King version, made popular again by her 2014 Tony-winning Broadway show, *Beautiful*. Others might think of Aretha Franklin's powerful rendition, which she performed at the Kennedy Honors for Ms. King in 2015. Is Aretha my inspiration? Actually, neither comes to mind when I break into song. I'm a child of the 1990s, and that big chorus line was heard over and over in a L'eggs pantyhose commercial. That jingle is inscribed in my mind, so I sing the only line of it I truly know. I serenade my love often. Doug's touch is intimately felt. I don't care what my medical charts say about paralysis.

Before I was married, the words from a former caregiver's dad often bothered me. This man once said to his daughter that he couldn't envision "Tasha ever having sex." I suppose this is where Ashlee's pop-up book could help! Finally, after gaining some of my own experiences as a married woman, I realize that some people will just never understand.

I do recall the information from Mayo's research that senses are heightened, aroused more, because what sensations remain are super-sensitive. Flashbacks to my rehab confirm this. When people touched the insides of my hands, ouch! It hurt. Early on, my mom shopped for softer washcloths for me. The bristly fabric of some hurt so much, I feared a good scrubbing from a caregiver would rub my flesh away. Super-sensitive. And in this way, my remaining nerve endings allow me to feel Doug's touch beyond what anyone can imagine. Of course, it's his responsibility to determine what feels best. And isn't that the joy in the process? Finding out what your partner feels and wants? That's the unselfish part of intimacy. And believe me, I feel more than ever expected—satisfaction beyond what some able-bodied people feel—because Doug and I are mutually attentive to each other's needs.

As much as I prepared for intimacy by reading and searching for just the right way to approach it, the answer occurred when sharing with Doug in the most open and trusting way possible. So, whether you have paralysis or not, focus on each other with affection, interest, and respect, and like me, you will feel beyond your expectations.

This brings me to Lesson #3: if it's in a movie, question it. One of my 2016 TashaSchuh.com blog entries panned a major motion picture summer release, and led to some significant Minneapolis and Eau Claire media attention. My blog, "I Am Not Suicidal: The Movie *Me Before You*," challenges everything from the lack of research for this screenplay to the inscrutable, suicidal end of a character who found love after his injury.

Doug and I cheered over the previews for *Me Before You*, touted as a love story between a quadriplegic and his caregiver. "Finally, a Hollywood movie for the masses, demonstrating that love and happiness can be found after life-altering paralysis!" Boy, were we misled. And disappointed. My blog entry expresses how our hopes were crushed by the fact that, in the end, despite this unique, loving relationship, Will, the main character, chooses death. As he longs for his former life, Will expresses the myth of the SCI again: his partner should find someone new who can fulfill her desires. Apparently, this means he should die and make room for that new lover. Hollywood got it dead wrong once again!

We were outraged, not because this portrayal was new to us. In fact, my blog references other films that get it wrong, too, like *Million Dollar Baby* and *The Bone Collector*. These stories capture huge box office revenues and influence millions of viewers who are duped into trusting a message presented by popular directors and cast members like Clint Eastwood, Hilary Swank, and Denzel Washington. Yet, despite strong, thoughtful main characters who have what it takes to face life after severe injuries, these films ultimately promote the misconception that disability not only steals your mobility; it steals your humanity. Paralysis will lead to despair and isolation, so life itself is not worth living.

Oh, these films will claim to show rugged individuals who exercise freedom of choice, who declare their humanity by taking God's plan into their own hands and opting to end their misery. But none of this could be further from reality. Just when some of these characters are on the brink of finding love and fulfillment after facing life's greatest challenges, they give up. Just when Will (ironic first name, don't you think?), the pensive main character in *Me Before You*, experiences true love, trust, and understanding from a beautiful woman, he gives in to some popular notion that unselfish love comes from letting the people we care about move on, that somehow Lou will be better off as a mournful, broken-hearted woman. Ridiculous!

A recent visit to one of my most cherished doctors validated my blog response, as well as the media attention it drew from both WCCO in Minneapolis and Doug's former TV station, WQOW.

Dr. Mark Christopherson, my rehab doctor, serving SCI patients since 1984, listened as I described my concern that media sources often get it wrong.

"Am I the only one who sees it this way?" I asked.

Once I shared my frustration with the latest Hollywood mishandling of SCI love and intimacy, I stopped to listen to a man whose life is dedicated to unveiling the myths which wrongfully influence his patients, as well as other SCI people throughout the world.

Dr. Christopherson literally said, "Who writes this crap?" Who writes a screenplay without the vaguest notion of a SCI person's inner concerns and desires? Good question.

"I can show you my PowerPoint, Tasha." Dr. Christopherson shared. "I take this everywhere I'm invited to speak. The stats tell the truth. SCI patients, with time to heal, are anything but depressed and suicidal."

Sure enough, the statistics speak a completely different story than what's conveyed by popular media. A Canadian study, respected as one of the most reliable, since all SCI patients in that nation report to one database—a result of socialized medicine—is most telling. Mayo professionals are mindful of these findings: 40 percent of SCI (C4 or higher) answer "no" to life in the first months of healing and rehab, indicating that they don't want to live after their injuries. Under a doctor's care anywhere—Canada, the United States, or any medical facility dedicated to helping SCI patients—such a percentage is disturbingly high.

Yet two years out—two years after recovery from their injuries, after rehabilitation and adaptations have occurred, after time for mastery of things like a tenodesis or a modified van, after a patient has settled into his or her new life—the percentages jump! According to the survey question, "If you can't walk, pee, poop, or have sex normally," do you really think you have a life worth living? Get this: 98 percent of SCI patients answer yes, as well as 92 percent of "high quads"—C4 and above. Unlike a Hollywood film created by people who seem to lack contact with the SCI world, Dr. Christopherson's shared research reflects reality.

I will admit: until I was married, I feared exactly what Will's character feared . . . that I wouldn't be able to provide Doug with the level of intimacy he desired. But these are normal, healthy doubts that come with being in a relationship. These concerns have little to do with one's disability. The joy is in overcoming these fears and finding fulfillment in the fact that intimacy is an ongoing challenge in a relationship. It can't be conquered; it is different every time you choose to embrace one another in your most loving expressions of closeness. How boring it would be if making love was exactly the same every time. So, once you finish a little academic reading, like this chapter on intimacy, pursue the truth in the old fashioned way . . . hold hands, look into each other's eyes, ignore the Cialis commercials, and find some private time to show your spouse what love is.

CHAPTER THIRTEEN

THE ART OF ACQUIESCENCE

I REALIZE WE ARE EARLY on in our marriage. However, if sharing what we've learned so far is helpful to readers, we'd like to do so without pretending to be experts. I gained insight regarding this from a former colleague of mine. I recall saying to her, "I can't give marriage advice. I'm too new at this."

She responded with this analogy: "Isn't someone with a two-year-old still a mother? She may not be a parenting expert. She's learning as she goes, right? But she sure can share what works and what doesn't. Just because her child is young, she's still a mother with experience to offer."

Well said, my friend. This convinced me that if I share what I am learning about marriage as Doug and I meet new challenges, someone might benefit. So here are some insights from a couple of newbies who are growing deeper in love with each passing day.

SIMILARITIES MAY BE WHAT ATTRACTED us to each other. Shared values definitely accentuate all that we have in common. Yet differences often rule the roost once a couple is under one roof. It may be cliché to say, but as a married couple, Doug and I definitely choose our battles. Every strong marriage, regardless of how good the private times are, depends upon communication, compromise, and acceptance . . . what I like to call the art of acquiescence.

Some things are not worth fighting for or over. The art lies in knowing intuitively—before conflict has a chance to even brew—that a difference of opinion, a different perspective, or a different way of completing a household task is just that, something different that doesn't validate a debate or an argument. Recognizing when not to fight is the art of acquiescence.

Doug and I are madly in love. Yet, immediately after the wedding, we confronted the difference between dating and making a home together. Twenty-four-seven companionship kicked in after the Door County mini-moon. Finally! Cohabitation with legal and spiritual marriage—we looked so forward to this! No more countdowns, no more long distance, late-night phone calls. Yet, despite our yearning for this stage of life, we quickly confronted some clues that "a period of adjustment" was upon us.

Suddenly, I was grateful for the prep work we did before the marriage ceremony. I had purchased two copies of a book by Gary Chapman entitled *Things I Wish I'd Known Before We Got Married*. This book laid the groundwork for open communication—a voice, without conflict—something every married couple hopes to have.

"Doug, I want us to read this . . . together. Our own private book club. What do you think?"

Doug looked at the chapter titles and agreed. "This looks awesome!"

We read one chapter per week in the months leading up to the wedding. Every chapter starts with the same words: "I Wished I Had Known . . ." and is followed by the chapter's title. The first chapter gives a glimpse into the wisdom of this book: "I wished I had known . . . that being in love is not an adequate foundation for building a successful marriage." Ouch. No fun! That sounds like the opposite of romantic love. But we both were committed to preventing what we had witnessed in marriages we thought would never dissolve. This book covers a range from some of the most predictable conflicts in marriage—that toilets are not self-cleaning—to the deep deal breakers that may lead to divorce and "that apologizing is a sign of strength."

I think the biggest takeaway from our book discussions was the need for ground rules. We knew that making a home together would be challenging for two grown adults who had lived alone. We each had spent years perfecting our individual methods of running a home—but those homes were for one. Now, complicate this with frequent entrances and exits from caregivers; the fact that most of my family lived within ten miles of my home; Doug becoming my employee, business manager, and acquiring some of my cares; and finally, Doug, to some degree, losing all that he knew of life in Eau Claire, including his church, his career, close proximity to his parents, and—maybe the hardest separation of all—his gym. This new life would need divine intervention or a leap of faith that comes with true love.

Ground rules, ground rules . . . what should they be? We both knew others who had conflicts early on in marriage, who had ongoing strife in their households, who started deeply in love but ended up divorced. What could we do to confront our differences—not hold back in silence and frustration—yet guarantee that our love, not our disagreements, would be the focus in our marriage? Now that we were finally together in one household, how could we have a voice to question and disagree in a healthy manner, without threatening the trust and support we valued?

The fact that we both wanted ground rules seemed like a good start. Now, to decide when to confront, when to continue the disagreement, and when to acquiesce . . . in other words, "to accept something you disagree with, without protest." This seems to be the key challenge: we must test our ground rules, not just create them. And some disagreements are not worth challenging.

Here's one I took on . . . something I believed required a "fight," from which I have now made a complete one-eighty. Yes, as hard as it is to admit, I was wrong! If our relationship had been built on a power struggle, on the ego of getting one's way, this might have been a bigger deal than it was. The wisdom gained from the art of acquiescence occurred pretty quickly for me.

So began the case of the disgruntled bride. The topic of dispute? Doug's gym time.

My husband has a history of personal fitness that started in his college days and flourished in his single years living in Eau Claire. He was new to Wisconsin back then, working many hours, and trying to pay his bills. Like so many young professionals, when he had free time, he had no cash to enjoy it. He chose to expand on his favorite hobby—something that would help him on the road to self-improvement: personal fitness.

Working out, whether it's cardio or weights, takes time. During those years as an Eau Claire area meteorologist, Doug worked and worked out. Add his active role in church, some weekly visits to his parents (who had moved from Detroit to Eau Claire in 2007), an evening here and there with friends, and that was about it. That was his life in the months before I met him. He became disciplined, found a routine, stuck to it, even pursued the thought of entering a bodybuilding contest in order to set new goals through competition. His nutrition changed, too. As he added protein to build muscle, he became very knowledgeable about the time and commitment it takes to sculpt a body to be in its best possible form.

And then he married me. Let's face it, my definition of "workout" is extremely different. At the start of my recovery, my fitness routine consisted of many painful physical therapy sessions on the small mat in Rochester Rehab. I went from a tall, lean volleyball player to someone striving for enough strength to operate my automatic wheelchair and modified van. I worked hard for those skills and have since added other tasks of independence.

However, when I met Doug, I realized fitness was a high priority in his life. All I had to do was look at him! I not only saw a sculpted body, but I witnessed the increased energy he had after his workouts. In our newlywed year, he was big and buff, and determined to maintain it.

Doug's commitment to health and wellness inspired me! I went back to my "arm bike" with a renewed desire to build some upper body mass. Unfortunately, this led to strained muscles. Apparently, my arms get enough of a workout from their normal daily use. My doctor informed me that overuse would only lead to more pain. So gym time backfired; it just wasn't going to be part of my world.

A high-protein diet fed Doug's fitness frenzy that first year of marriage.

Protein is a quadriplegic's favorite formula to maintain energy for daily work and to accelerate healing when skin wounds occur. Still, our diets and definitions of fitness were miles apart. Sure, Doug's "guns" in that T-shirt got my attention back when we first met. Yet, now, as the wife of this fitness freak, I began questioning the number of hours per week he spent at the gym.

I also worried that Doug's concern for a buff, hard-bodied look would translate to him wanting me to look like the bodybuilding girls he saw at shows. Would I eventually disappoint him because I lacked that look?

"Just so you know, I am never going to be able to look like those women. Even my upper body—the parts that work—can't develop muscles and definition like you have. We won't be working out together. That's not something I can do."

"I know that," Doug responded. "And I wouldn't expect you to, even if you could. It's my thing, but I wouldn't ever expect you to be into this."

Whew, that was a relief. Yet, there was a period of adjusting to the fact that Doug would have a hobby I could not share in.

Doug was intense. For instance, in a week without speaking engagements—when we were not traveling or acutely focused on prep time for a presentation—Doug needed eight to ten workout hours to maintain an acceptable level of fitness. Four or five days per week, a couple hours per day . . . this was his noncompetitive, maintenance gym-time when we were first married, which, as mentioned, has changed. But at the time, we had to confront this part of his lifestyle. At one point, Doug truly thought I would be okay with him driving a ninety-minute round-trip to exercise at the nearest LA Fitness!

Since that first year of marriage, reality gradually changed things. Time is a luxury. We have both acquired so many more responsibilities as our business has grown. Doug now spends less time on workouts—a change he chose when bodybuilding lost its allure. If you met Doug at one of my presentations in the past year, you might think, "Hmmm . . . he looks fit, but not bodybuilder big." In the past year, Doug changed his regimen and focus. He's after energy, a leaner look, and improved cardio now. In fact, he's lost nearly fifty pounds this year! Yet I will always recall this as a major point of contention in our first months of marriage—one which could have threatened our happiness had either of us disrespectfully dug in our heals.

I get it now, and ironically wish Doug had even more time for the gym if he still wanted it. Right after the wedding, however, I used our ground rules to question the time, the cost, and the hours away from home which this activity required. Suddenly, I found myself analyzing the hobbies of other husbands . . . hunting, fishing, motorcycling, antique collecting, golfing, boating on the St. Croix River. These were costly hobbies as well. Yet I found myself, like a defense lawyer, prepping my argument against Doug's commitment to the gym.

I reminded him, "I don't mind that you spend that time without me. Besides your morning hours at the gym, our day is pretty much spent together. This is a healthy way to spend time apart. Every couple needs that." But the hours his workouts took away from our work schedule concerned me.

Finally I realized that Doug wasn't Doug without his hobby, because it wasn't just a hobby to him. It was a lifestyle. Fitness had become a part of who he was. I didn't need to be the nag who deprived him of a healthy pastime that made him tick . . . that gave him energy and happiness and confidence. We had great debates, and with time to observe and listen, I acquiesced. Now, some years later, I am completely supportive.

Thus, when Doug's a little irritable, after we've been on the road or had a full weekend of company, I find myself thinking, "He needs to get to the gym." I think that's code for, "Please get your fix; I want my Dougie back!"

In the process of this fitness debate, we began to analyze my own hobbies and interests. What was it that made me tick? What passion did I possess, with or without Doug, that allowed me to be fully Tasha? Doug's discovery put me on the defense once again, but I no longer try to deny it: my hobby is work.

"You're a workaholic."

What? Me? No, that can't be true. I love leisure time—movies, dinners out, family gatherings.

But Doug asked, "What's the one thing you do—the activity you go to when you don't have a plan? What's the first thing you think of in the morning? How do you fill free time when you should just be appreciating the moment?"

"Work!"

It was true. Checking emails, reviewing a speech I had already prepared for, worrying about details that had long been established. An overachiever syndrome had kidnapped me. Perhaps it stemmed from those years in college when I refused to let my disability interfere with my goals. And soon after graduation, a fear of failing as I started my own business took hold of me. Likely, those years of not dating fed the passion for work, too, as I filled a void with business tasks. Regardless of the reasons for this pattern, filling ten hours mostly at my computer . . . reading, researching, ruminating over work already completed, triple-checking items that may or may not have needed my attention . . . all of this was easy. I love my work!

I made time for my nieces and nephews, often said yes to lunch with a friend, pitched in at church . . . did lots of fun things over time. But when I was home, I was working. Every free second of any given day.

Now, I had a new life. My obsessiveness had established a degree of success which I honestly don't regret. However, it was time to change. Doug's observations were spot on. I needed to adapt and find a new balance. Acquiescence again.

Our ground rules included some basics, like don't be reactive. Instead, observe and then openly share. Even when it seemed critical or harsh, this process helped us both (and continues to) find compromise and mutual respect for each other's personal passions. Fortunately, we both possessed hobbies or pastimes each of us could accept.

Through our discussions, we both came to believe that early problems in marriage could be avoided by analyzing our leisure-time choices. Acknowledging the need for private space and time could build some balance into the family schedule. And as a family—because that's what we are now, with or without children—we needed to define that experience while still respecting each other's individuality. A close analysis of how we spent a day before marriage helped us determine how to alter this, now that two were under one roof.

Gary Chapman helped, too. His website and book about the five love languages made us both aware that we had very different ways of looking for evidence of love. My first love language is physical touch, and personal affirmation is a close second. I love Doug's touch, as well as his kind and attentive words. Doug, however, requires a different love language to fill his tank; he needs quality time—my undivided attention. In those early months of marriage, when I finished supper and then scooted into the office to work into the evening hours, Doug put his foot down.

"Whoa, wait a minute. Where are you headed?" Doug asked. I thought it had something to do with the fact that I wasn't able to help him do dishes. But he was actually trying to stop my workaholic ways.

"You're done. The workday is over." Doug stressed the need for us to be "home" together, just the two of us focused on one another. His love language showed me I needed to be attentive—I had to be present—for Doug to feel loved. And, clearly, we both benefit from filling our tanks this way.

Our ground rules, however, do not guarantee we can always dodge a fight. Yes, as much as we hope to avoid the proverbial domestic dispute, we'd be lying if we said we never argue. Raising one's voice, showing impatience or disapproval with a spouse—these things prove we are human and have our limits. But deciding what a fair fight looks and sounds like has been a ground rule discussion worth having.

Some might wonder, are the physical differences at the root of all our marital differences? If we have a disagreement, is it because I am disabled? Not at all. The fact that I am an extrovert and Doug, while social and friendly, is more introverted has caused more ground-rule debates than anything else in our marriage. Simply put, he prefers more alone or quiet time than I. Therefore, the lower level of our home has morphed into his office and workout area, a quiet place for reading or resting, a.k.a. the Man Cave. And I have learned not to commit both of us to every social invitation that sounds inviting to me. These are common adjustments all newlyweds should make.

Yet the need for extra people in my life, caregivers who professionally and personally give their time and talents so that my life is richer and more fulfilled, cannot be ignored. Doug saw this while we dated and has always followed my lead on how much and how often caregivers entered our time together. Some have become my close friends. This aspect of our private lives will likely ebb and flow for many years to come, so flexibility and open communication will be needed again and again.

CHAPTER FOURTEEN

BUSINESS AND PLEASURE JELL WELL WITH DOUG MICHAELS

W E WEREN'T EVEN ENGAGED, and already Doug was openly questioning his role in my cares and in my life. No other boyfriend had ever inquired so thoughtfully yet so matter-of-factly.

"So do you think that someday I'll do your cares?" Doug asked one evening after a scheduled caregiver finished her shift.

That was easy to answer at the time: "No. No way."

"Why not? I mean, I'm not questioning your choice of answer—just curious why you think I shouldn't." Doug was so objective and knew few of the details of my shower, bowel, and catheter cares at this point.

"I'll tell you what I have told my parents and siblings," I replied. "Personal cares become a burden to a family. There's unnecessary stress whenever these kinds of cares have to be done. It's one thing to be a backup, like all of my family has been over the years. But those years of Mom, Dad, and Angie doing almost everything for me—well, that just wasn't sustainable. I won't have someone I love do that for me, and I will always pay caregivers—even if they are family—to do things I can't do."

Again, Doug accepted my lead on this subject. However, since that talk, we have experienced those times when waiting for a caregiver just didn't make sense. No other aspect of our married life has experienced more change than this, now that the full scope and scale of cares have been revealed to Doug, and now that Doug has acquired full management of my business.

With all that he does for and with me now, I have to think hard and long to remember the days when I believed I could leave Doug out of it all . . . when I preferred to shield him from the inventory of duties that came with making life as a quad seem normal.

"Why can't I just transfer you into bed?" Doug asked one night at my house, after dating for some weeks. I could see that his confidence in observing my cares was growing. But I continued to insist on secrets—that he not learn every little detail of my personal cares. Some things were better left unsaid. In this situation, he acquiesced—for a while.

But time has a way of unveiling secrets, and although that first year of the Ms. Wheelchair USA Pageant had me hiding behind closed hotel doors, the second year in Ohio was a much different story. And if you recall, my caregiver and I shared a room in Grand Marais with Doug, the weekend of the proposal. With wedding expenses already on Doug's mind, this was a money-saving plan to which I did not object.

Thus, by the time we were living under one roof as man and wife, the caregiver schedule had been slightly reduced. Doug encouraged me to accept his role in some household chores, especially cooking, consequently saving on daily caregiving expenses that might be saved for the overnight speaking budget.

Steadily, unforeseen circumstances taught us both that, in a pinch, Doug can do just about anything my disability requires.

1. "A NIGHT AT THE WILD GAME" BECOMES "OVERNIGHT AT THE HOLIDAY INN, ST. PAUL." DECEMBER 2013.

Despite his enjoyment of hockey, Doug becomes the unofficial Director of National Weather Service before we venture out to a hockey game—all because of one wicked weather night. A week before Christmas, we happily set out on "date night" to enjoy one of Doug's favorite sports. Although the game was exciting, more drama unfolded as we returned to the parking garage after a Wild win.

Our van failed to start.

My van is vital to my mobility. Over the years since my accident, I have driven three. People often think there is "support" for all adaptive equipment. And sometimes there is. I secured financial assistance for two of my vehicle purchases. Fund-raiser money after a benefit can also supplement the high price of a wheelchair-accessible van. But this was my third vehicle and by far the most expensive.

My first vehicle was funded partially by DVR, the Division of Vocational Rehabilitation. They paid $20,000 for my gas-and-brake system installment, lock-down system, and a few other things needed to customize this used van to match my abilities. I paid the other $20,000, which was the difference in the price. Over time, when I needed a second vehicle, since no assistance was available, I had all of my specialized equipment transferred from the first van to the next one. Even reusing the specialized equipment, the grand total for my second van was still quite costly—$42,000.

By the time I required a third vehicle, that original gas-and-brake system was no longer valid. We discovered that the technology was outdated by three years, and I was required to buy all new specialized equipment—plus the new van itself. Because my gas-and-brake system is so complicated, the conversion experts said up front that they would never be able to transfer this new combination over to a future vehicle. Thus, when this van quits, I will need to repurchase everything again, with no assistance.

I am grateful that DVR helped me get started back in those days when Dad took the time, and the risks, to teach me to drive. This cost-sharing gave my family the confidence to pursue my desire to drive. And once a person gains the independence that comes with owning and driving a vehicle, there's just no going back. As it is for most working and commuting Americans in this spread-out land of ours, a vehicle's expense is a necessity of life for me. Therefore, I spend lots of time and money maintaining my van. Let's just say the mechanics know me well.

For anyone newly disabled and interested in the independence that comes with driving, you should know that your level of paralysis dictates your vehicle's needs. Since my arms are so limited, I essentially had only one option. Considering career demands which have me driving all over the country (although I always seek the cheapest accommodations possible) some unavoidable expenses come with my level of injury. My gas, brake, and steering system, with a computer record of everything I do when in the driver's seat, is unique and quite costly. However, this system, which allows my weak arms to put on tens of thousands of highway miles required for my job as a professional speaker, is a must. Audiences don't come to me; I must go to them. And, since many of my driving months include the potential for rain, snow, and ice, I need the safest independent system possible.

In addition, I require a make of vehicle which doesn't have a history of mechanical problems. Think about it. If my van doesn't start, I can't jump into someone else's car for a quick lift home. A Good Samaritan can't rescue me from the hassle of a stalled engine. I am glued to my wheelchair, which weighs 350 pounds without me. We are inseparable, my chair and me. A tow truck can't haul my van to just any local mechanic. Plus, I would be left behind without a ride. Being stranded and looking for roadside assistance is a pain for everyone, but it is truly a disaster for me.

So the autumn before meeting Doug, I searched for the most reliable minivan on the market. DVR's policy for adaptive brake and gas equipment helped again. I realized I wouldn't receive any financial assistance for any future vans, so when I learned that this electronic gas-and-brake system—a whopping $40,000 this time around—was nontransferable, I purchased what I believed was a van with great longevity—a Honda Odyssey which, after accommodations, would exceed $100,000.

I know I've taken all the precautions I can to ensure that my van is reliable. But even with a very accommodating and highly trained Twin Cities mechanic, I've had a few break-down experiences. Not often, but I think it's true what they say—the more bells and whistles, the more things that can potentially go wrong. So although I know I made the right purchase, even with the sticker shock, vehicle worries always sit in the back of my mind.

That night at the Wild game, Doug and I knew we were stranded. Even though someone helped us by offering to jump the battery, the van continued to stall. At midnight, we gave in and called a tow truck.

I recalled seeing a Holiday Inn close to the stadium as we were heading back to the car. We ventured down five or six blocks to spot the hotel but found the doors locked at this late hour. We noticed four inaccessible steps to the first entrance and an intercom button.

"Hello, there," Doug blindly greeted the front-desk attendant after pushing the button. "Do you have any rooms available tonight?"

Suddenly my husband's good manners began irritating me. It was nine degrees Fahrenheit, and my teeth chattered uncontrollably. I had no gloves or hat, and my skin was starting to burn from the cold.

"Let's just get in the building, Doug," I urged in the background. "We can negotiate the room in the lobby—the warm lobby."

I felt like we were Mary and Joseph—*Are there any rooms in the Inn? Please don't turn us away!*

The hotel employee informed us that the accessible entrance was around a corner. I felt so grateful to come out of the frigid Minnesota night into a safe and secure building. And yes, they had a room for us! But when Doug looked at me, he could tell I feared spending an entire night without something essential left at home.

"What's wrong?" Doug read my face. He figured I was worried about the van and spending an unplanned night away from home. "It's just overnight. We'll be fine."

"My Baclofen."

"Oh, oh—the Baclofen," Doug sounded worried, too, but not as worried as me. We both remembered that I had used the "emergency" stash of Baclofen from my backpack on a recent outing but had not taken the time to replenish the supply. My nighttime dosage of my antispasm medication was ritual for me ever since those sleepless nights of jumpy legs in college.

"I don't know how jittery my legs will get tonight." When my legs get spastic, my bed vibrates as if a train were coming through the room.

"It'll be a quick night. We have to get up early to check on the van. We'll get through this," Doug reassured me. He knew sleep was important—for both of us. Completing my cares in an unexpected time and place would be difficult on minimal sleep. I sensed we would cross that bridge when we had to, the next day.

In retrospect, I am grateful for these "oops" moments in our lives. How else would we learn anything new? We made the best of an emergency situation as I trained Doug to help with my cath cares, and he got me safely into bed. The next morning, we completed some vital cares, which got me by until our return home. Whew! With the van battery replaced, we headed back to Ellsworth to regroup with a hired caregiver.

Our growing sense of couplehood created confidence for both of us that Doug was willing to do whatever I asked of him. Although I was gaining faith that he would not feel burdened or taken for granted by this, I cautiously kept my stand that Doug should remain the backup. I thought that he could do cares if he had to, but we were never going to plan things this way.

"But how am I ever going to get good at it?" Doug asked one day. "I mean, if I am only the backup, it'll never be routine."

It was true—my caregivers completed their tasks with skill and efficiency because of repetition. So, Doug made the valid point that he would eventually become more adept at the task if he helped me more frequently. This would minimize the stress when a caregiver called in sick, or some other emergency, like van trouble, popped up.

2. "WHAT HAPPENED IN VEGAS DID NOT STAY IN VEGAS: INSPIRATIONAL SPEAKING ENGAGEMENT AND LESSONS LEARNED WITHOUT A CAREGIVER." MARCH 2014.

"Here's a perfect situation for us to practice doing cares on our own." Doug's suggestion met my skeptical looks, but he went on to persuade me to try this brief, overnight trip to Vegas as an exercise in self-reliance. I was booked to speak in the evening, so we would jump a plane in the late morning and return home the very next day, with minimal cares needed on the road.

"No caregiver," Doug stated. "Not on the flight, not for the hotel night cares, not for the morning prep before we go home."

I did not share his enthusiasm.

"We can do it! Come on, trust us."

Doug reviewed all that we had to do. So, sure enough, we flew in late in the morning for that evening presentation. My biggest worry—my hair, something I will never be able to do on my own—was completed by my caregiver at home, before departure for the airport. I can get two days out of Britney's hairstyle skills.

"I think that if you weigh the energy and attention it takes for three people to travel together, it's not any more stressful or time-consuming to travel just the two of us." Doug sounds so reasonable, doesn't he? Why should I question his willingness to help? Wouldn't this minimize the cost of travel since he, not a caregiver, would do all the cares?

Keep in mind that a few factors made me very cautious in accepting these caregiving changes: Doug had never done cares for any family member—not a grandparent, not his parents, not even an aging pet. Up to this point, his life just hadn't presented such experiences to him—experiences like I had in my childhood when I spent weeks in the summer helping Grandma Barringer with cares for Grandpa, whose weakened heart triggered his physical decline.

In truth, I didn't want to overwhelm Doug. Plus, I valued the ease at which an experienced caregiver could do what she was paid to do. Yet Doug insisted. He was eager and persuasive. I honestly don't think I could have prevented this step in our lives. So the next step in our relationship got started, and we began taking trips on our own.

3. "OUR FREEDOM TRAIL FOUND IN BOSTON—FREEDOM FROM BRINGING A CAREGIVER, THAT IS." APRIL 2014.

Doug wasted no time; he convinced me that our speaking trip to Boston, which was precisely one week after Las Vegas, should be done without a caregiver. Doug knew very well this trip would be four days and three nights away from home. A big city, a demanding schedule—the ground rules were tested again. So, before departure, we planned ahead, and Doug learned the "long cares," which was code for my most private procedure, my bowel care program.

I was mortified by the thought! Doug, the love of my life, the man I spent hours primping for in our dating days, whose romantic attention I always want, would perform the SCI version of toilet tasks! My intuition knew he was right about this, but my feminine insecurities said, "No way!"

"Let's start training now," Doug said, "and by the time we return from Vegas, we'll know if it's a good idea or not."

The Las Vegas trip would not require long cares, but other challenges would reveal themselves. Challenges like hauling luggage through the airport—consider all the extra clothes and supplies we must take on every trip, just in case—missing that extra set of hands provided by a caregiver when traveling, checking into a hotel, dining, and securing transportation in a strange city. Vegas would teach us so much.

We prepared for these long-distance events, training Doug as the one and only caregiver. His job had evolved into so much more since he first left the TV station weather center. And his role as my husband tore down boundaries I thought would never be broken.

I acknowledged a new trapdoor—one I had strategically placed in my defense of privacy. But this trapdoor was providing privacy from a man who had done nothing but love and support me. In the weeks preceding our trips, as I let Doug into my most private world of quadriplegia, I felt like I was falling again. I feared I would hit the floor and realized I had shared too much, expected too many cares, scared my husband away. But unconditional love has a way of cushioning a fall, building trust, and deepening love.

Boston could have been a short visit, like Vegas. But, Doug, an avid student of history, insisted we extend our stay.

"We can't fly to a city like Boston without touring," he pointed out, then rattled off a list of sights he hoped to see while on the East Coast. We were also fully aware that the one-year anniversary of the Boston Marathon bombings was later that month, so April felt like a poignant time to visit.

I love history, too. Yet, considering early spring temps, especially in a breezy, coastal area, I questioned how Doug would do all of my cares, plus haul enough sweaters, blankets, and hats to keep this freeze baby warm. I wanted us to enjoy, not just endure, a touring extension after my speech commitment.

I admit it—my hair is one of my biggest worries when on the road. I can do my makeup, but my limitations prevent me from styling my own hair. The solution in Boston: cute hats! Suddenly, I was grateful for the cooler weather. My caregiver prepared my hairstyle for the Boston speech, which I gave on the departure date of the trip. By day two, however, I had Doug pull out a hat for me. I was warm and ready to roll, to and from every historical location and restaurant on our itinerary.

Our biggest concern of the trip turned out to be the Boston taxi service. Anyone traveling in a big city can typically count on a wheelchair-accessible taxicab service. People like me can't enjoy the usual Hop-On, Hop-Off tour bus convenience. So Doug and I budgeted more for transportation during our extension in Boston. Sure enough, we found the designated area at the airport for wheelchair-accessible taxis. However, from the first ride to the hotel until we left the East Coast, we risked my life in very unsafe vehicles. Each consecutive ride to see the Boston city sights seemed to get bumpier and more dangerous. I had never encountered a wheelchair-accessible minivan that I didn't fit into. This was very dangerous!

Boston cab companies advertised their compliance with the ADA, yet they only provided vehicles with minimal accessibility. None of the transportation companies offered a minivan with the head clearance I needed. So, when Doug inched me into the back of the van, the door couldn't close because of my headrest.

"Maybe we should have them call for a full-sized van. We'll just have to wait," I suggested.

But after Doug requested a new van, the driver informed us, "This is as big as they get."

"I have been all over the country. I've used taxi services in multiple cities, and I've never had a problem with my wheelchair fitting," I answered.

The driver actually agreed with us. "We run into this all of the time. The minivans follow the state compliancy requirements. So that's all Boston requires of the cab companies," he explained.

Doug and I acquiesced and put this in God's hands again. We prayed every time I rolled into the back end of one of these tiny vans. Since we had to remove my headrest to get me in, my head was literally against the window of the van's back door. Upon every bump, my head hit the glass. Doug was buckled up in the front with the driver, so I know he was unaware of how scary this was for me.

"This can't be ADA compliant," I said to Doug.

"The entire city cab service does this," the driver said. "Sorry, but these vehicles are compliant to the state of Massachusetts." He must have meant it when he said this happens all the time because he certainly had an answer ready to counter my concerns. But he was genuinely worried. Every time we hit a bump, he was watching in the rearview mirror to see that I was okay.

An awkward van ride in Boston.

I was so frustrated, but what could I do? *This can't even be legal.* My anger was interrupted by prayers for safety as my head hit the glass again. I had such a crick in my neck from having to turn and hold my head cocked that I wondered if I would need physical therapy after the trip! My head had to be turned and slanted to one side to get fully in the back of each minivan.

Despite a few bumps in the road, Doug and I learned again that so much could be accomplished if we work together.

4. "SPRING BREAK? MORE LIKE SPRING TRAINING!" MEXICO 2016.

Could we go it alone for over a week in a foreign country? A last minute emergency had us both questioning a trip we had planned for months. The morning before we were scheduled to leave, our spring break caregiver was diagnosed with influenza pneumonia. We had two choices: we could lose the money we spent for our caregiver to accompany us to a lovely Cancun resort but still take the trip, having Doug do all of my cares. Or we could opt out completely, stay home, and lose everything—the trip, the cash, and the vacation time away from our Wisconsin winter.

Our caregiver felt terrible, but she was coughing up blood and knew that leaving the country would be too risky. At this time, she was our one and only worker who possessed the level of freedom to travel for more than a week. Our other employees had second jobs, college or high school classes, or children of their own. A free trip to Mexico, although tempting, just isn't feasible for most of my employees. With less than twenty-four hours to search, we considered filling her airline ticket with someone—anyone—else. Realizing we couldn't transfer the ticket to another name, we made a quick decision: we would go anyway. Alone, we would pack it up, board the plane, and prepare for eight days in paradise.

It started out rather rough. We spent about half of the vacation wondering why we were there. The convenience of home is hard to give up. Routines are in place, caregivers are scheduled, things run like a well-oiled machine.

At the resort, things seemed new and hard again. When I'm out of my accessible home, everything is out of reach. I need so much more help. I was constantly asking, "Doug, can you do this?" I had to rely on him for so much. I felt like I was nagging, and I started to feel like a burden. But we overcame the learning curve. When two people work together, attitudes can flip quite quickly. So, by the second half of spring break, the vacation we had hoped for kicked in.

Here's what we learned in the first part of the week: we both allowed worry to dominate our days. I worried that Doug would lose his patience with the long cares. Doug worried that if the long cares took too long, we would both be exhausted the next day. I worried that Doug's lack of sleep would make him hate Mexico, a tropical climate I loved. Doug worried that although this was his vacation too, many hours per day were spent doing cares—essentially "working."

At about the halfway point, reason and perspective edged their way in. After one very long night when bedtime cares went into the wee hours—two thirty, to be precise—we both realized that we had survived a most stressful situation. We lived through it! No one died from lack of sleep. Neither of us collapsed from too much worry. And the cares were still there, nothing had changed. Except our attitudes. With a few days remaining in this tropical wonderland, we both made an unspoken decision to focus on the warmth and beauty of the beach. We unconsciously, without judgment, completed the cares that had to be done. With grudges gone, our anxiety lifted. We loved Mexico so much that we vowed to visit again—hopefully every year!

The fact that my mother and her friends stayed at the same resort helped us immensely. Mom volunteered to do my hair each morning. She—along with Jeanie, Ken, and Linda—probably had no idea how they helped Doug and me snap out of any anger and resentment built up from the challenging cares we faced back in our room.

Whenever we revisit the ups and downs of traveling together, Doug always comments on how much we have grown as a couple due to these trips that test us. I don't ever want to take this for granted. I love and admire Doug even more when he says he has been "pushed out of his selfishness." Caring for me, he says, has lifted the veil of his own private world which came from living alone. I adore him for saying such things, although at times I think he is too hard on himself. But love does challenge people to a level of care for one another—a level we maybe didn't know existed.

In fact, it took me a long time to trust in that level of love. So when people ask me, "Do you and Doug ever argue?" I have to answer, "Oh, yes—for sure." For example, don't debate with my hubby when he's tired and hungry. We each have those times when we are overwhelmed with life and say something unfair to the person closest to us. But I want to make one point about Doug very clear—our marriage is successful because he goes above and beyond what is expected of him.

Doug comes in every morning about three minutes before my caregiver arrives to start the day. He crawls back into bed after unlocking the door for the scheduled caregiver and lies next to me just long enough to tell me how beautiful I am, how much he loves being my husband, and that he "can't wait to serve" me for the day. He initiates the steps for my morning preparations to begin once the caregiver arrives. He reminds me of Ephesians 5: "Husbands, love your wives, as Christ loved the church and gave himself up for her . . ." And more than anything, Doug reminds us both that if we focus on each other's needs instead of what each of us wants, or what we can get out of the relationship, fulfillment will be experienced. Saint Francis of Assisi said, "For it is in giving that we receive."

I find myself wondering, *So what did I do for Doug today? Am I part of an unbalanced relationship? Will he get tired of this? Will it become a routine?* He has laughed at me when I ponder over how I can repay him for all he does for me every day. He reminds me that marriage is a commitment, and few couples find a fifty-fifty equation to keep fairness at the forefront. So why fight over things that can't possibly be even-steven? Doug sides with one of my friends, Andrea Hanson, who truly lives the movie *Me Before You,* although hers is with a continuously happy ending.

I knew Andrea's husband, Chad, years before they met. He had survived a bad car accident one night driving home from college, and I was called upon to pay a visit. This was a little over a year after my own accident. I touched base with Chad a number of years later by asking him if I could tour his newly constructed home to see his floor plan. I looked at Chad's house for design ideas, since he had beaten me to the building process.

Months before this, I took time to visit a former caregiver, Shelly, who was close friends with Andrea Hanson, a student I knew at Winona State University.

"Hey, I think Andrea and Chad are an item," Shelly said to me that day at lunch.

"What? Chad and Andrea?" I was utterly confused, since I had no idea that they even knew one another.

"I'm as surprised as you! I knew that Andrea had applied to be a caregiver for Chad, but I guess one thing led to another, and these two have fallen in love."

Yes, Andrea was her husband's caregiver when they fell for each other. This is the stuff of movies! Yet no one is more authentic about being married to a man in a wheelchair than Andrea Hanson. She knew from being the caregiver first all that this lifestyle would entail. And nothing intimidates her. Someone once asked Andrea point-blank, "So why did you pick a spinal-cord-injured guy?" Andrea shot back immediately, "He chose me. And I'm so grateful!"

One of my favorite posts from her blog, something she shared on Facebook after being bombarded with questions like "Don't you get tired of doing everything?" shows Andrea's remarkable perspective:

You know what one of the best things about being married to a guy in a wheelchair is?

It's not the rockstar parking everywhere we go, nor is it all of the adorable questions that small children ask when they see his chair. Those are great! But what I love goes much deeper than that.

I am responsible for all of the house chores.

Whoa, what?! Yup, this is actually a perk in our marriage. If the floors don't get cleaned, windows washed, laundry done, I have zero bitterness in my heart.

Some women have frustration boiling inside, wondering why their husbands can't help around the house. The fact that Chad cannot help me do any of this, means we don't struggle with who is going to do what.

There are dishes in the sink? That's all on me. Dust on the end tables? Again, my fault. The only person I'm allowed to be frustrated with is me! Imagine all of the arguments that we avoid because of this. I consider that pretty darn lucky.

I was blessed with this by default, but you can also have this type of freedom in your own marriage. Talk to your spouse about what each of you can do to keep the house running. Chad does all of the bills, grocery shopping, and entertaining Mari while I am busy cleaning up.

Neither of us struggles with thoughts like, 'When is he/she going to help more with ___?' Disappointment and frustration stem from a lack of communication. Talk. Talk to your spouse about how you can serve them better. If we all served our spouses, what a wonderful world we would live in!

Side note (with picture of their adorable daughter): Now that's not to say this cute little lady isn't going to get out of helping mom. Her time is quickly approaching.

Andrea's insights help me so much when my Beth Moore wisdom steps backward every now and then. The words from the husband of a very good friend come racing back occasionally. This guy once said, "Why would Doug sign up for this? I don't think he could really possibly love her."

This question and comment sting! As if he challenges Doug's intentions, or wonders if Doug is in it for the long haul. But when I take inventory of all Doug does for me, for our business, for our home, for my family and our caregivers, I am reminded of the proper response to this man's words: because Doug loves me.

Doug has not only learned how to be a skilled caregiver; he also manages the kitchen, including grocery shopping, cooking, and cleanup. He completes much of the laundry, taking care not to shrink my many warm sweaters and blankets. Doug maintains our yard until the first snow flies. He does give our niece Anna a chance to earn some money for college by cutting the grass sometimes, but he nevertheless oversees trimming, weeding, and all the other lawn care.

Within the office, Doug manages almost all of the budgeting. This includes financial stuff like prep for our personal-income and property taxes, tax items for Tasha Schuh Inspirations, LLC, as well as payroll and documentation of W-2s for all of our caregivers. He utilizes Quickbooks and spreadsheets, where he tracks IRS-required deductions, profits, and payouts. His calendar and scheduling management includes recordkeeping for all our bookings, from the initial point of contact through the actual event. Doug does some cold emailing, reaching out to a school or business, for instance, if we are going to be in their area for a different presentation. This type of multitasking as we travel is routine now for Doug.

Driving to and from Dallas this past spring—fifteen hours with a few stops—brought our caregiving issue full circle. Doug performed all of my cares on trips to Mississippi, Tennessee, and Dallas. The shortest of those trips was four days, and the longest was eight. Conclusion—he can do it all! But, from now on, he won't. The driving alone is a massive obligation. In a five-month span, Doug drove 215 hours. Hence, we will hire a caregiver for our longer road trips.

Some people have suggested, instead of a caregiver, why not hire a driver? But Doug enjoys driving. Getting in and out of the van is easy for me. Readers can check out my videos on my YouTube channel to see how my van accommodates my wheelchair. "Join Me for a Ride in my Van," posted in 2015, explains the technology of my customized van and actually shows my step-by-step procedure to drive myself, without assistance from Doug or a caregiver, which I mastered in those years before my marriage. Doug at the wheel, however, rounds out our travel demands perfectly since his willingness to drive frees me up for extra prep time. This reserves my energy and focus for each big event.

Doug wrote his own reports as a meteorologist, so his composition skills contribute to our business, too. In addition to collaboration on this very book, Doug is often my second brain if I am struggling to compose emails or if I am questioning my wording for any written document. He proofreads, gives me feedback, cowrites some blogs with me, and assists with my vlogs.

I try to fulfill requests for products that might advocate the uplifting message I share. People said, "Why don't you write a book?" So I did. Now we hear, "When will you write another book?" So we did. Others asked, "Do you have T-shirts or mugs or bracelets?" People know these items are talking points. These items help spread the word and remind them of my message. Since some of my audience members prefer to go home and shop online, Doug took charge of the mail service for these products when ordered electronically. This definitely increases during holiday time, but orders are steady throughout the year. Doug tracks our inventory, reorders for resupply, and brainstorms new designs when people inspire a product change.

End of tally sheet. I could go on, but Doug doesn't particularly like it when I take inventory of the many things he does for us. Maybe it reminds him how busy he is! Most likely it makes him feel uncomfortable since he is not in this for anything but love and the hope of helping others by positively impacting lives. He will often remind me of my independence, and how I accomplished much of this profession without his presence for quite a few years.

In the early days of my career, I often traveled without a caregiver, if the mileage was reasonable. I could drive myself, make my presentation, and depart in time to make it home for end-of-day cares. If I worry that I am becoming too dependent upon Doug, he will sometimes remind me of our first dates; there was no caregiver in the van when we met for coffee or dinner in Menomonie or Eau Claire.

It is important for me to acknowledge that Doug's role has increased because of our business's growing demands. I think back to the months when my first book was released, when we were a new couple and Doug was still very tied to Eau Claire. I received the first shipment of my first book and promptly recruited a volunteer friend to travel with me to public library appearances, book signings, and other community events that showcased *My Last Step Backward*. Since Doug was still a meteorologist, he only had limited time to help with book sales. He shared many weekend hours in this, but during the week, I needed to recruit someone else for a helping role.

Enter my friend Mary Klaustermeier. She was so happy that my book had been published, she offered to help in any way. Recently retired from public school teaching, Mary taught part-time at a community college where I had presented to her students. These were young adults who, despite some setbacks, were now reentering the world of postsecondary education. Mary worked around her teaching hours to clear her calendar and accompany me for book-signing events throughout much of 2013.

At the St. James Hotel in Red Wing, Minnesota, Ginny Houck walked in, listened to my introduction to a story in which she had an integral role, then talked with Mary Klaustermeier while I signed books for others.

I was thrilled to see Ginny, who had driven all the way from Mazeppa, Minnesota, to see me. If you read my first book, you may recall that Ginny, my primary care nurse while in the ICU, literally helped save my life when I became so sick. We had a great visit! We vowed we would get together for lunch soon, and I thanked her for the support in coming to one of my book signings.

It wasn't until I was back in my van with Mary that I realized how much of my own story I still did not know. While I signed books, Ginny shared details with Mary of her memories of my struggles and successes after my theater accident.

"Tasha, wow! I had no idea how bad things were," Mary commented as we headed home that night.

"What do you mean? You knew I spent time in ICU," I replied.

"Yeah, but I had no idea how close to death you were. Ginny gave me the details of one night where she was sure you were not going to survive. The respiratory therapists bagged you for hours!" Mary said.

Later during that busy year of book sales, Ginny paid us that visit we vowed to make. As we sat around my dining room table catching up, sharing new milestones in each other's lives, the conversation came back to those days we spent together in Rochester. She was with me when I slipped to the other side—when I crashed and the medical staff of St. Mary's thought I was gone.

Ginny narrated like it happened yesterday.

The doctor was stepping out of the room when Ginny said, "Hey, come back here. Just look at her for a minute. Her sats are dropping. She just doesn't look right."

The doctor came in and agreed.

"There were three of us there—the respiratory therapist, the doctor, and me. The doctor decided to do a bronchoscopy; he wanted some medicine to go down the tube. But when they put the medicine in to start the procedure, well, that's when you crashed," Ginny recalled. "I remember looking at the monitor about ten o'clock at night. I couldn't even read it."

"Wow, this is crazy. I didn't know any of this," I said.

Ginny explained that my lungs, so tight from the trauma due to septic shock, would not even ventilate.

"We started to bag you."

"What?" I interrupted. "Remind me what that means."

"Two guys hand-ventilated you until about one o'clock in the morning. Your lungs got stiff. They just couldn't be ventilated. So they had to manually bag you as long as it took. I don't even know what to really call it. You didn't officially flatline. It was just a real crisis."

I couldn't believe what I was hearing.

"Then we had a lot people in the room! The residents, the consultants . . . there just were a lot of people squeezed into that tiny corner room of yours," Ginny added.

I hung on every word Ginny conveyed. These were details I know my parents don't even know.

"Dr. Harris, a pulmonologist, stayed there with me and the ICU team all night. He only left the room once—to change from his suit into scrubs," Ginny continued. "Oh, and the order came for central lines right away. First, they did the quickest one they could—in the groin. They had to get meds for blood pressure going." I could tell Ginny was trying not to forget anything. "We had the meds ready to go, but then your heart rate dropped. I was all set to do CPR—I had my hands on your chest and was almost starting to cry—but then the heart rate went back. I just had to keep it together."

"It sounds like everything was changing so fast that you didn't have a chance to lose it."

"You've got that right!" Ginny replied.

Ginny was so heroic that night, but she downplayed it even when she revealed how hard the whole experience was.

"Somebody brought me a glass of water at one point," Ginny explained. "Later, when I turned to drink it, it was gone. Nadeen, the other nurse, looked up. 'I was thirsty too!' We got a chuckle out of that."

"What? You never even took a break for food, a snack, some water?" I asked.

"No," Ginny replied. "I left for work at six fifteen at night. I didn't go to the bathroom until the next morning when I got home. I didn't have any fluids either, so I had no reason to go to a restroom anyway."

"Wow. That's a long, scary shift, Ginny. Amazing." I was grappling with my own emotions while she talked, but the sacrifice she made that night was right up there with the shock of realizing how close to dying I was.

Ginny reminisced about that night, as well as the many times she cared for me and her thought drifted to her own daughter. Erica, Ginny's daughter, was one year older and also a tall teenager. "You two are the same height," Ginny explained. "I'd see those long legs, and I'd think, 'Wow, this could be me.'" In other words, Ginny knew she could be the mom now dealing with a daughter this sick—a daughter who had so much healing to do before she could even begin to adjust to this new life.

"Remember Dr. Harrison?" Ginny asked, as if to change the subject slightly to a less dire topic.

"He was from Australia, I think—amazing accent!"

I think we all had a crush on this charming white-haired man. Age didn't matter; he was amazing.

"Oh, yes," I replied. "He was always a favorite." He kept a watchful eye on me for quite a while after this incident.

"He made sure no one moved you for three days. No CT scan, no other tests. You were just too unstable to move, for anything," Ginny explained.

Ginny continued to talk about how hard this was to convey to my parents. "We told them, 'She's really sick.' But your folks had so much faith in us. In fact, another nurse told me later that Kathy"—my mom—"said, 'Oh, we know she's sick. But Ginny's in there. She'll get her through this.' I mean, your parents really did not acknowledge just how sick you were. How could they? I mean, people have to have hope."

To lighten things up again, Ginny explained the silver lining in one of her most stressful experiences in forty-seven years of nursing.

"I was supposed to update my CPR skills that month. But when the state tester came around, after hearing the full story from the staff, she said, 'I think you passed!'"

"Okay, I gave you that one, Ginny!" I was struggling to know how to share my gratitude for all this woman did to save me. I was again grateful for her sense of humor, which helped me listen and endure the most dramatic story about myself that I'd heard—that I was so close to missing out on the best years of my life.

Ginny's perspective reminded me how close a call I had, and that I wasn't exactly an active participant in my ICU experience. I had no real memory of this dire time. And since none of my family was in the room when my body actually crashed, nobody knew all of these details. I had never truly conversed with Ginny about these things.

Revisiting my miracle, my reentry into a changed but beautiful life is so important. I'm grateful when Doug reminds me that I navigated so much of this change on my own, as an independent woman, before meeting him. This is so important to hear.

I marvel at Doug's patience and acceptance of a wife who will never be able to even the score. I try. I tell Doug, every day, how much I appreciate him. By complimenting him on all of the work he gets done in a day, his cooking, and everything else that contributes to our lives together, I believe my words make a difference. Doug sees that I give back in other ways, too. My gifts to my husband are not conventional. For instance, while recently visiting the Lundvalls in Wyoming, Ashlee and I arranged for Doug and Russ to have a full day free for four-wheeler riding in the mountains.

Doug had never ridden an ATV before. So the time and experience meant more than any "thing" I could have given him.

Despite my limited movement and strength, I have figured out a method to give my husband a massage. Well, massage is not the right word for it. By lightly tickling Doug's head, arms, hands, and feet, Doug experiences a touch therapy that is so different from anything experienced from a paid massage therapist. He loves taking a break from the physical work around the house for this.

I gave him a T-shirt that displays the phrase "Best. Husband. Ever." He loved this gift! Clearly, I can't repay Doug; I can't even the score. But what couple can? We all bring different gifts to the ones we love. As long as we are mindful of our spouse's need to be appreciated . . . as long as we make the effort to remember how blessed we are for the love and support we receive, I think our partnerships will be strong. Suddenly, "evening the score" will have no purpose. Doug challenges me to be a better wife, and by doing so much—knowing I can't take my turn at dishes, laundry, or cooking—his love transcends equality in our relationship. People like Doug and my friend Andrea live this wisdom every day in their married lives.

With all of the things Doug does, you can imagine why I now insist on taking a caregiver on all trips—especially for those non-work-related vacations. Yet, get this: Mexico, spring break, round two. One year prior, we had struggled through and decided this spring break would definitely include a plane ticket for a trusted caregiver. But, after weighing the gains from traveling on our own, we deliberately chose to depart for our second spring break to Mexico with no extra caregiver. Let the adventure begin!

Mission accomplished! Another milestone! Going it alone was, okay, doable. However, this was spring break, vacation. We both think a trip like this could be more leisure—if only a caregiver accompanied us.

This experience, along with tens of thousands of miles in the van for a very rigorous winter-spring speaking circuit, has convinced us: Doug should have help. He wears enough hats on this mission to spread my story. We thoroughly enjoyed speaking engagements throughout many southern states, where the warm weather provided an added perk for this freeze baby. However, experience is a great teacher. Going forward, we will train and include caregivers to travel with us for both business and pleasure. Doug knows absolutely everything now, and he can do my cares if necessary. But our marriage is strongest when he sticks to being my husband and my partner.

So, in early June, Doug and I made it a priority to find a caregiver to join us for Wheelchair Camp in Stewartville, Minnesota. Doug kept busy helping others and overseeing my participation for this event. The people attending the National Wheelchair Sports Camp are of all ages, sometimes new to the wheelchair way of life, and sometimes veterans of wheelchair use. Doug not only enhanced the trip for me but for every participant he met. If I can show them how happy I am, if I can cheer them on in their activities, if I can help them realize that the best of their lives is yet to come, my mission will be complete.

Without a doubt, Doug facilitates all of our travels, oversees our home, and manages our business in ways that cannot be listed on a job description. He goes above and beyond the call of duty as he helps navigate my goals and monitors my time. Doug notices things I would overlook—he's my extra set of eyes—and he does all of this so effortlessly. Although it would be possible to complete these things without him—as my friend Ashlee often says, we were independent before we met our husbands—I know my impact as an inspirational speaker is so much greater with his presence.

One thing is certain—Doug and I thank God for the gift of life and the gift of our relationship. For me, so many of our experiences together have proven that this man really loves me! I'm the type of wife who says forget the roses or gifts, girls. When a man truly becomes your partner in life—when you know he intends to be by your side as you accomplish your dreams—then you know you are loved.

CHAPTER FIFTEEN

THE QUESTION OF MORE DROGORUBS

WHEN THE SCHEDULE PERMITS it, Doug and I find we are content to stay home. Over the course of presenting fifty to seventy times per year (which is the average for any able-bodied professional speaker, by the way), we fulfill our desire to travel. We've become the quintessential "old married couple"—minus the old. We love simple things like a home-cooked meal, a date night close to home, and a small campfire on our deck.

"Do you two get sick of each other?" my niece Isabel asked one day. Having two jobs with us—working as a caregiver and a marketing support person in my office—Isabel spent lots of hours per week with us before she left for college.

"What do you mean?" I asked.

"I don't know," she replied. "But sometimes my friends will say, 'Don't they get sick of each other? Working together on the road, and then, being at home working together?'"

Doug looked up from whatever pile of paperwork he was sifting through to answer this.

"Nope," he butted in. I smiled and let him finish.

"Isabel," Doug continued. "Think about it. I had thirty-six years of my life to be alone. And eleven of those were totally on my own. Don't you see how this was what I was looking for? I had alone time. Being with Tasha all day is what I was waiting for all my life."

"Okay," Isabel replied. "Don't get all romantic now."

Doug came in for a kiss, and I was happy to give him one.

We welcome people into our home every day . . . caregivers, business support people, family, and friends. But we both enjoy our private time, too.

Doug and I definitely notice how content we are when we consider the next natural step in a loving marriage: Do we want to have a child?

That question comes up almost every time I present. And quite frankly, our answer has wavered somewhere between "yes, soon" and "we really aren't sure." After some months of marriage, we decided to approach the idea more earnestly. We confronted the medical side to childbirth first. Some thorough research into how a woman with an SCI carries and delivers a baby was essential.

To my surprise, I found the medical world had updated perspectives on this. Until recently, I thought I had no choice but to deliver via cesarean section. But a discussion with my physician's assistant had me considering a natural delivery if I chose to get pregnant.

"Really? For some reason, I thought that because I wouldn't feel the labor pains, I would have to schedule a C-section."

"Well," she explained. "Imagine what an epidural does for a mom who feels everything. It takes much of that away by providing pain relief. We don't want the anesthesia to completely eliminate feeling. But we know that the body would take over—just as it would for you. Labor begins, you dilate, and baby comes naturally. Some quadriplegics have elected to do this."

"Do some end up in surgery anyway?" I asked.

"Yes. But I want you to be aware that the option is available for you to consider."

Doug and I appreciated her information. Yet, in deeper discussion, we both knew that our hesitation to have a child was less about the delivery options and more about our family's future.

We had just become a family—found each other after both wondered if we would spend our lives alone. We love what we have! We feel a calling to do what we do, sharing my story in hopes that others benefit and feel inspired to search for their purpose in life.

And neither of us will have a child simply because it seems the natural next step after marriage. We are not going to have a baby to prove we can have a baby.

I recall people reacting with pity years ago when I would say, "No, I'm not married." No matter what chapter of my life I was living, that expressed disappointment bugged me. While dodging a relationship, I would think, *I can have a great life without a man!* When on the lookout for a husband (definitely less frequent), I would think, *Gee, give me time! I am not settling for just anybody!*

Now, I finally understand the reaction most people gave me on the topic of marriage. I love being married so much that I understand that these comments weren't always pity—just people wishing the best for me, wishing I had what they had. I get it! Marriage is awesome!

I now feel that little pang occasionally from others who ask, "Will you have kids?" Because lately our answer is, "No. We don't plan to have children. We don't see how they would fit into this busy life we have together."

However, when asked, "Could you have children?" we consider so much more than just getting pregnant, carrying the fetus to full term, and enduring delivery. Those steps mark the start, the tip of the iceberg, for a very big, lifelong commitment. Sure, the SCI issue throws a bit of a curveball into the situation. Yet after discussing this as much as we have, after considering how weighty the job of parenting is, a commitment to expanding our family seems out of touch with the path we've been taking.

Having a child is a big initial step in parenting, but by no means the most important consideration. With modern baby gadgets and gizmos, caring for an infant is quite possible, and fairly common, for a parent with a spinal cord injury. Modern conveniences facilitate the experience for infant and disabled parent—things like attachments to a mom's wheelchair for feedings, infant seats that allow a toddler to ride on the wheelchair safely, or a slew of other items that guarantee a mom like me could bond and care for the baby.

However, Doug and I see the bigger picture and realize that so much of parenting occurs after the baby stage. We just don't believe this is the path we've been called to take right now, especially with our busy speaking schedule. Until we feel differently, we will continue our lives by loving, honoring, and lending support to those who have chosen to take the parenting path.

I've learned much from hosting sleepovers for my nieces since they were very young. Although the girls are now older, Doug and I continue to lend a hand when my sister and her husband take some much-needed vacation time without their kids. These childcare experiences—albeit with nieces I adore—provided a glimpse of all the intricacies of raising children. However, our current mission to help others, through a business which has grown substantially since we married, would have to change dramatically if we decided to have a baby.

I consider my friend Ashlee Lundvall an excellent parent. She and her family came to visit recently, darling daughter in tow. Doug and I asked, "Can we just have her? Can't you just share your adorable daughter with us? Maybe forget to load her into your car when you leave."

We knew the answer to that. Ashlee and her husband, Russ, have experienced a lot of love from Addison, yet they have also invested a lot of work into their child. She is a joy to be with because they have given of themselves: time, love, patience, and consistent discipline. And because she is so young, the real work is still ahead. We have full faith in the Lundvalls to continue to be the strong parents that they are.

Like so many people we know—Angie, Ryan, their spouses, our parents, and many of our friends—we respect and admire the challenge they have accepted to be parents. When a child enters the picture, everyone is impacted. We know that our loved ones would support us if we chose this path. Yet, to date, we feel the call to continue the life we have started with our marriage. Doug and I have a different purpose, a different focus. People may have expectations for us, but having children is not going to happen unless we feel that this is indeed in God's plan for us. We value our marriage, and we value what we've been called to do.

As a woman with a spinal cord injury, I often wonder where I would be on these heavy issues if not for the friendship and support I've experienced from Ashlee Lundvall. She gets it; she lives it. She loves her life, too. She supports me in my endeavors in more ways than she knows. Her perspective is so relevant because, as she lives the SCI life, too, she knows precisely when it is a nonfactor. She knows and helps me see more clearly when love and marriage have little to do with a wheelchair or a list of cares.

Take, for example, a conversation Ashlee and I have had more than once. We both have encountered a common, courteous response that accompanies the "congratulations" upon hearing we are married.

"Oh, that's so great that you found someone. It takes a real special man to be willing to do this, someone who will help care for you. He must really be something."

"Sure is. I'm so glad I took one for the team," Ashlee will usually reply.

This last part often stops people in their tracks and really gets them thinking. She does not let this go. She sees it as a teachable moment to dispel a myth.

In other words, Ashlee has a wonderful way of turning this stereotype around—the preconceived idea that her husband, Russ, settled. That maybe he's one of those guys who was deliberately looking for someone to serve and care for, that he must be making sacrifices and compromises that other husbands aren't willing to make.

Ashlee takes the conversation a step further by stating, "I married my best friend, not a caregiver. Russ respected my independence; that's one of the reasons he was attracted to me. I was already very self-sufficient. Sure—does Russ make things easier? Absolutely. But doesn't your husband do things for you? I'm sorry for you if he doesn't. Russ certainly makes things easier, but not possible."

Ashlee and I often share that, although people care and want to understand, they don't get how hurtful it is when they say, "I'm so happy you found someone. Your husband is so special."

Ashlee's quick comeback also includes, "Shouldn't we all be looking for someone special? Didn't you marry someone special?"

The first time I overheard Ashlee challenge someone on this, I asked her, "What if you offend them?"

"It's important to get them thinking," she replied. "You can do it with a sense of humor, and most will see pretty quickly how my sarcasm actually broadens their perspective."

I think this is especially true when Ashlee pokes fun of the "perks of partnership" that Russ gained in marriage to Ashlee.

"Number one: great parking!" Ashlee jokes. "Ha! Russ called home during his recent business trip and complained about the event parking."

Ashlee explained how he had to walk quite a distance to find a spot for his car for the day. "So, without me along, no disabled parking spots for you!" she reminded Russ on their phone call that evening.

"I was quick to remind him," Ashlee declared to me. "I'm so glad I took one for the team. I married you so you can have great parking!"

≈ CHAPTER SIXTEEN ≈

YOU ARE MY HANDS, BUT I SHARE MY HEART

FROM THE FIRST TIME he asked if he could help transfer me from wheelchair to sofa, Doug entered my world of caregiving in a gradual way. I know couples who make it work—where the able-bodied spouse is the number-one caregiver. But since that is not my goal, Doug entered my world of caregiver management respecting the system I had in place.

Some people have asked if the atmosphere for my caregiver team changed once a man joined the mix. Frankly, after our wedding, after Doug moved in, he sincerely added to the positive culture already found under this roof. Doug is welcoming and conversational, and he helps or stays out of the way—whatever the tasks require.

I wanted Doug to know why I interview, hire, and sometimes have to fire caregivers. In other words, Doug didn't really question the difference between using an agency versus hiring my own crew; I wanted him to know the history of how I got to this place where I am the "boss." In retrospect, I am thankful that many of the early lessons of managing caregivers occurred before our wedding, so the dynamics of our marriage were never really impacted.

Doug said he noticed right away that my home provided an atmosphere of comfort in which to work. Once a personal care assistant (PCA) learns the rules and demonstrates she can meet the expectations, we enhance the experience so it doesn't overfocus on the "work." We listen to music, we talk, we joke around, and we develop a mutual working friendship. Most of my caregivers say, "It's hard to call this a job."

Consequently, most PCAs leave work feeling uplifted and encouraged to take on the day or face whatever personal struggles they may have with renewed optimism. I can't say enough about those who have accepted this job and performed at their best. You know who you are. Past or present, you know when you are good at this job, when things ebb and flow, and when we complete tasks with minimal anxiety and mutual respect. Some of the best have not been able to commit for very long, while others have been with me, steadily or off-and-on, for years.

Although I try to state it every day, my gratitude, expressed or unspoken, is endless. And for those who have moved on to other careers, marriage, or children who need them at home, I hope you always feel the satisfaction of knowing you did a job with skill and compassion and made a difference in my life.

The Old Tasha Schuh never dreamed she'd be the boss of anything more than her next role on Broadway. I knew from observing my parents that hiring and firing, payroll, and accounting were for business majors who wanted full responsibility for their own business. Then gradually, as I sought out the best people I could find to assist me with my personal cares, I acquired all of the tasks that accompany the business of managing a group of PCAs. I learned from experience how the art of being the boss could make or break the quality of each day.

I admit, while I am welcoming and appreciative, I have "my way" of wanting things done. I have had years to discover the most efficient, comfortable, and collaborative methods of getting ready for the day, or night. I want caregivers who will honor this.

At times, an applicant—anyone with a pulse—is next to impossible to find. Other times, the talent pool of compassionate caregivers is abundant. For a short time, I posted ads, but I rarely found what I was looking for in a caregiver. Once my speaking career took off, people became aware of my situation. Word of mouth still works the best. It enables me to consider the recommendations of close friends or family.

"Hey, I think so-and-so is looking for a part-time job. She's so hardworking. Why don't you call her?"

One thing I shared with Doug right away were the stories in which I had been betrayed in the past. These experiences made me passionate about finding and keeping the best PCAs. If there is one message I can share with Individuals with SCI, it is that you deserve the best care. For far too many reasons, I tolerated poor-quality workers, and although I have conquered many of the what-ifs as the New Tasha Schuh, I have some regrets about being too patient or too nice with caregivers.

"Why would you put up with that?" Doug asked. "If someone is unreliable, why wouldn't you terminate her right away?"

"I believed I had no choice," I replied. "Because I offered only part-time hours to employees, and because I paid less than a healthcare facility" (although this has changed). I feared I wouldn't be able to find a replacement. I don't think I told Doug this, but because Beth Moore's wisdom was sometimes blocked by deep insecurities that accompany paralysis, I tolerated some horrible traits in a few of my caregivers.

I remember explaining to Doug a decision I made in college. For a while, I used an agency for caregiving services, as I believe most people who require cares will do. But soon I started to seek, interview, hire, and supplement the caregiving schedule with some of my own hires.

My motivation to freelance was twofold. First, an agency charges you hefty hourly fees; they have to. Consider the wages needed for the caregiver, then add the HR duties involved for services provided at a great volume. The many overhead costs of the agency require income enough to balance the books, maybe even show a profit, depending upon the agency ownership.

Secondly, I had some rather negative experiences with agency PCAs. I can't speak for all agency hires, but in my college town—Winona, Minnesota, where I first started using a service—PCA workers from the agency were not always quality people. Reliability issues made me question the level of screening being done. For example, my very first agency caregiver stole from me, lied on her timesheets, and even forged my signature.

For months, I paid out so much unearned money because I did not realize this was happening. Contrast this with personnel back in Ellsworth—people who were my friends, or friends of my family, in a small town where everybody knew your name.

I was so hurt when I discovered the truth about this first agency caregiver. How could someone do that? It made me question the management and their screening process. I was automatically suspicious of the next PCA they sent over. This was my experience, but I have talked with others who wouldn't do it any other way. The convenience of an agency works for some. But I did not want to continue working with an organization that seemed well aware of this problem but did nothing about it.

I saw many reasons to question the integrity of this setup. Besides the thief, I had been burned with too many no-shows. Tardiness, too, caused me tremendous anxiety in college. A late caregiver meant I would miss the start of class. Imagine the apprehension of watching the clock, wondering when she would walk in, knowing full well that, without being upright in my chair, I couldn't do any task on my own to make up for lost time. And then I had to refrain from blowing up once she finally arrived because I needed her cooperation to get me out the door ASAP. Who had time to fight about it?

Ultimately, my disappointment was with the agency more than with the employees they sent me. I had the benefit of being surrounded by some very trustworthy young women—Brooke, my high school friend and college roommate, for one. So I began to rely more on my own connections from Ellsworth who were Winona students, and others I met as I navigated campus life.

In addition, I really liked one caregiver from the agency who was super reliable. She confided in me about how frustrating her own agency experience was from the employee's point of view. She started a little freelancing herself. She quit her job and began picking up hours directly from me. This initiated my transition into being the boss of my own caregiving staff.

I never looked back. However, change hit after college graduation, when I returned to my hometown. Many of my trusted caregivers in Ellsworth had moved to new towns, new jobs, and new lives. I was starting over, and building a new caregiving staff was far from easy.

I felt like a rookie again. Insecurity crept in, and I started to tolerate poor caregiving traits. Since I was so independent for the level of injury I possessed, I never had long, full-day shifts to offer a worker. I thought I had to ignore some shortcuts from my new PCAs. I forgave those times when a caregiver canceled and left me stranded or when a caregiver disrespected me because her own personal life was in crisis. For example, one woman called in sick frequently and always at the last minute.

"But I only need you for an hour and a half. Then the rest of the day is yours." I think her most memorable call went something like this: "I can't come in because my daughter quit breathing."

Really? She quit breathing, yet you took time to call me? I think you ought to call 911. I wanted to say this, but instead I supported her and said, "Take care of your daughter. I'll find someone else." And then my calls began. I had to beg someone else to change her plans. I would have to ask another PCA to drop what she was doing to help me. I hated it! But what choice did I have?

At least she called me. There were numerous no-shows. They worked for a while, and then poof! They quit coming. They wouldn't answer their phones. I was devastated the first few times this happened.

I helped them; I trained them in with kindness and patience; I let them into the most intimate aspects of my life. And they left me hanging so many times. Even on the day of my grandmother's funeral, one caused me heartache.

One woman worked for me for nine years and had arrived a few times drunk to do my cares. I suspected . . . and then I knew. Yet, like one half of a dysfunctional relationship, I was in denial. I kept thinking, *You are the only one who knows my bowel care program.* But I would block out the truth. One of the oddest situations occurred when she found herself in a relationship with a man who was jealous of our friendship. He resented her dedication to me and became so irritated with it that he finally said, "You need to show that you love me more than Tasha." I'll never forget one Easter

Sunday . . . my mom was hosting our family gathering, and this woman texted me to cancel my evening cares.

Doug and I were engaged at the time, but I was trying my best to camouflage the challenges that came with caregiver dependency. Doug, or any member of my family, could have helped me. Yet I felt compelled to prove to everyone that I had things under control. I saw her text message and privately called her, hoping to handle this without impacting our holiday meal.

I begged her to reconsider. By this point, I had definitely become more assertive with last-minute calls.

"You are putting me in danger—do you realize that? There is no one available to do your shift. People shouldn't have to change their schedules on a holiday." That night, with her boyfriend prodding her in the background, she simply quit.

These situations caused me so much anxiety. I teetered between feeling like a burden, feeling anger and resentment for being abandoned, and feeling I would have to beg and plead just to get to bed safely at night. Incidents like this reinforced the very thing that I fight all the time . . . that my survival depends upon others. I can't get out of this. I can't climb into an able-bodied suit for the night to go to the bathroom, to change out of my clothes into pajamas, to brush my teeth and crawl into bed for a good night's sleep.

I felt trapped!

These very situations prompted my bad catchphrase habit. I am notorious for saying "I'm sorry."

My closest friends, my family, and now Doug have called me out on this. For a while, every other sentence was "I'm sorry." People began pointing out that I should save the phrase for the rare times I actually do or say something wrong.

So many times, I've been confronted with rebuttals like, "Sorry? Sorry for what? Sorry for needing things you have a right to as a human being?"

One friend told me to knock it off. "Why do you say 'sorry' so much? Sorry for what? For being alive?"

That hit a nerve. I had not realized how prevalent and how symbolic this phrase was. Yes, I had to admit, sometimes I felt sorry that I had to ask for help for so many things. But I was often on pins and needles, thinking my caregivers could find new jobs at any moment. Saying "I'm sorry" was my way of taking the blame for asking them to do something for me, even though they were being paid for their time.

Now add this to the catchphrase list: "Will you do me a favor?"

A few new caregivers began to call me out on this one, too. "Do you a favor? Why do you say that? I'm working for you. I'm on the clock. These aren't favors—they are duties and tasks outlined by the job."

Thank God for sincere employees who see things this way and draw my attention to this awful habit, a habit I haven't conquered yet. I see now how it devalues me. I demote myself and trade my place as boss every time I say such phrases.

Eventually, I hired a caregiver with the same habit. It drove me crazy! It made me realize that this was my method of approaching a problem, of empowering others by suggesting I was wrong. But it clearly created a new problem. Consequently, I needed another phrase to explain away more feelings of insecurity.

"Just love me." This catchphrase passively allows me to request things to be completed as I want them. If a caregiver questions a routine or a task, I apologize but ask her to still do it as requested. "Just love me" is my way of saying, "I might be wrong, but do it my way, please." This self-deprecating phrase helps provide a shortcut. I bypass any discussion or analysis, yet I don't have to sound like the boss. I avoid phrases like, "Don't ask me, just do it." This may be my nice way of asserting authority. However, it some-times backfires. Passively stating "I'm sorry" may empower an employee to think she has authority over me.

These are some of the experiences that made me want to hire and train my own caregivers. It was frustrating to be questioned on routines that are simply about who I am.

For instance, when questioned on daily tasks like skincare, I admit my facial routine is time consuming. Some might even say high-maintenance.

But isn't it a personal preference? A caregiver who never wears makeup to her job might be tempted to ask, "Why do you feel the need to use these products? Why use different skin creams? What's the point of putting on makeup every day?"

When this occurs, and it has frequently, I am tempted to say, "If you had a career in public speaking, you might empathize." But I am always cautious. If a caregiver has a different point of view, I have to let her know, "I don't have a choice. I have to put on makeup in the morning, because I don't know if my day will require a need to look put-together. If someone calls and says, 'Hey—do you want to go to the movie,' I can't just decide later in the day to get ready. If someone pops over unannounced, I want to look prepared for the day." Wanting to feel confident in front of hundreds of listeners at a presentation is just part of my concern for taking care of my skin.

Another part is that I am very acne-prone. I have been since my accident. The trauma of my fall triggered a change in my body chemistry that shows up when I am stressed. (This was extremely evident when my last boyfriend prior to meeting Doug broke it off!) Preventing breakouts, protecting my skin, and addressing this sensitivity have to be priorities for me. Therefore, the different products used in my daily regimen and the time they take to apply are worth it!

"Just love me." In other words, quit questioning me; I am a grown adult. I know what works. You've been hired to assist with personal cares. Just work with me—and please don't make me analyze my choices. I wonder if some caregivers know the many interpretations of my favorite phrase.

My mom is a living example of how skincare pays off. She is always put together and looking beautiful. Much of it is her attention to using sunscreen and daily moisturizer for youthful skin. I want that too! Just because I need assistance with the application of such products doesn't mean I should have to compromise my hopes for graceful aging.

After the most notorious experiences with caregivers, I documented some changes. Some discussion with Angie helped me pin down a few principles which continue to guide my confidence as employer.

1. I can provide a list of expectations for any caregiver, any employee who enters my house, and she will honor that list.

"Write an employee handbook, and if a caregiver can't live by the rules of the job, let her go." Angie's advice, delivered before Doug came into my life, led to a solid business practice, which I will never change, in the caregiver management world.

In this document, revised and updated as needed, PCAs will find:

Page 1: A letter of introduction, starting with "Dear employee, I am very excited that you have chosen to be an employee of mine," and concluding with a directive to read and abide by the handbook thoroughly.

Pages 2 and 3: "Standards of Conduct," which include a code of conduct regarding everything from reliability to open lines of communication to grounds for termination.

Page 4: Confidentiality/Employee Agreement. This must be signed by the employee to validate that the agreement is clear and acceptable.

2. I do not have to retain caregivers with personal or professional flaws that threaten my safety out of fear that they cannot be replaced. If an employee doesn't work out, I am the one who must let her go. No one likes to fire a worker, but I personally prefer having this responsibility instead of turning it over to an agency that may feel understaffed and therefore willing to let poor workmanship drag on until the caregiver in question can be replaced. These conditions were long in coming; I just hope I can help a SCI reader steer clear of similar hardships.

Caregiver dependency: I have cried and cried over the need to have others assist me with personal tasks that most people just do and never have to think about. I still felt a cloud of worry over this, even after Doug entered my life. He encourages me to be firm with caregivers, and this helps me build confidence in my role as employer. Our partnership means we are both invested in training the best workers to come into our home, to support me as I navigate this busy life. Yet Doug, too, has questioned my ways at times.

Some of this is typical newlywed stuff. When two people move in together, they are bound to say, "Hey, I do it this way." It might involve the laundry detergent I prefer, or the way I like my bedsheets left untucked. For a disabled person, these subjects become very personal. I sometimes feel lesser than others when challenged on these choices, even when it's coming from Doug.

"Hey, Doug, will you please . . ." As a wife, I never want to sound like a nag, but Doug gets constant requests from me. It just comes with spending so much time together. But when Doug disagrees with the request, most often joking, I feel something I don't think would be there if I had full mobility. An able-bodied wife may find an alternate way to fulfill the job. She is empowered to do it herself. I don't have this choice.

"Ugh. He forgot to take the garbage out. I'll just do it myself." This may be irritating, but the job gets done. However, I can't be the backup person for house chores. I don't have the option to do the garbage.

Garbage is probably a poor example here. Doug is one of those rare guys who has always been awesome about the garbage. In fact, the big house chores are never the issue for Doug. His many years of independence taught him much about maintaining a home.

Requesting the little things is actually when I have felt like a burden to my very able-bodied husband. Adjusting my backrest, filling my water cup, changing the fan to a lower setting—this list of daily needs makes me think twice before I ask Doug again to help me.

"Honey, will you get my sweater in the bedroom?"

"Nope."

Okay, this was a joke. Doug's unique sense of humor.

But his little jokes were suddenly bugging me. When turned down, even in jest, Doug's words impacted me. He thought it was funny. I didn't. It was wearing on me.

At first, Doug didn't see this. He didn't understand that every time he disagreed with me, I felt I had no recourse. I felt like I had no authority.

He rolled his eyes a few times to indicate disapproval, then laughed it off. "I'm just kidding!" Then he would do whatever I was requesting. I tried to see the humor in his sighs of effort, or his eye-rolling as he got up from his chair the second or third time to retrieve something for me. But the bottom line was that his small reactions were building up inside of me to the point where I had to tell him, "Please stop. This makes me feel like a burden."

Doug disagrees with me. He believes that I should never feel like a bother. He insists that I should never question my need for assistance, but as caring and empathetic as he is, let's be honest; he cannot imagine what this is like. Anyone dependent upon others for this level of care and mobility knows it's not a good way to feel, but there is no way around it. I can't change my dependency on others, so I must acknowledge it. I must confront it. And Doug encourages me 100 percent on this point. Needless to say, he rarely teases me for my little requests. In fact, I think he jumps to do things, just to make the point that I am loved and nothing I ask for is a burden.

Before Doug came into my life, I had Angie to mentor me on the right way to interact with my caregivers. When I confided in her, Angie always advised me, "Tasha, you are the boss. This is a business. You are not their friend. Don't put up with this."

Doug and Angie's support proved to be so important the year I suspected a caregiver was stealing from me. I feared it, but I found it so hard to prove. I discovered later, from another coworker, just how twisted this situation was. The thief actually bragged to a few people that she had been stealing from me and told them how easy it was.

In retrospect, I also wondered why my wound never healed with the wound vac on under her watch.

I recall my doctor saying, "This should be getting better. I don't understand why it isn't healing. You're not even sitting on it."

This dishonest caregiver was the only employee at the time who was able to attend doctor's appointments and trainings with me to learn how a wound vac worked. She knew how it attached to my wound to heal a skin breakdown which I couldn't feel or even see. I accepted her willing attitude to help me. To my face, she was helpful, positive, almost a cheerleader.

Behind my back, she was stealing, cheating on hours, and possibly doing things to endanger me.

For a time, this employee had me convinced I would have to overlook missing cash, food, and other household items, because she was it—the only caregiver I had to fill some rather unique hours.

Ultimately, I had a camera installed to catch my thief. Funny how she chose to quit a few days after the camera was mounted.

I will never again tolerate the emotional roller coaster that comes from caregivers who don't have what it takes. I will pay more for a solid level of proficiency, but regardless of the minimal hours, I expect caring, dedicated, reliable help.

I admit, the learning curve has been huge. Many of my preferred techniques have evolved due to negative experiences. I used to be transferred to bed, for example, without the Hoyer lift. I fought that thing. Consider the feeling of being over six feet tall, dangling in a hammock, up in the air, hoisted overhead, from wheelchair to bed. My fear of heights magnified the experience! So for years, I insisted on a transfer board, as long as it worked. A couple of pinch injuries from the board, however, left me with wounds that changed my attitude. A busy life meant I couldn't afford the time to heal. I couldn't take a chance with the board any longer. So a Hoyer lift became a permanent part of my transfers.

And when I say an "old" Hoyer lift, I mean "manual." This lift used a crank rather than push-button technology.

Fortunately, I upgraded to a Joerns® lift a few years ago. Joerns, the company that now sells Hoyer lifts, transformed my life! They gave me the opportunity to try a new lift after an encounter while speaking for a company that truly values quality care. I was speaking at Diversicare's Annual Leadership Conference—this is a senior-care company with which Doug and I have fallen in love. After my keynote presentation, I helped with another session on seating and positioning. During the Q and A section, someone asked me, "What do you use to transfer?"

"Currently? I use the Hoyer lift." I proceeded to describe the metal, hand-crank model positioned near my bed back home in Ellsworth.

When the session was over, a lady approached me. She was stunned at the fact that my lift was so outdated.

"No way. You don't have an electric Hoyer lift—a push-button power lift? That's just not right," she stated.

I was aware that power lifts existed, but anything with push-button technology was super expensive.

That was when Loren Martin, senior director of Loss Prevention from Diversicare Management Services fully introduced herself. "This has to change. As busy and productive as you are, an automatic lift will make a big difference in your life."

I explained why I hadn't gone there: my insurance covered the hand-crank model, but a new lift is upward of $10,000. I used one when I went to the doctor's office and saw them in hospitals when visiting other patients. But I had never pursued one for my home. I just couldn't justify the cost.

I was thrilled at the possibility of trying one!

"Oh, it may be a used lift, but it will bring your transfer into the current century. As active as you are in your life, you need a power lift," she stated.

Two weeks later, Joerns called me.

The Joerns people heard my story from Loren and were amazed at all I had accomplished.

"We are sending you a brand new lift to try—not a used one. It'll be shipped to your house."

The next thing I knew, the Joerns representative who called my home was flying in from Pennsylvania, just to train my caregivers on all of the features of the new electronic lift.

The sling for this unit is entirely different—definitely more secure. A caregiver simply pushes a button to raise or lower me—talk about safe for the PCA, as well as for me.

With the old lift, I always had one fear: if a PCA released the knob too fast, I would abruptly drop down to the bed, which, unfortunately, happened more times than I want to admit.

When the replacement lift arrived, I discovered that I possessed the original Hoyer lift—the oldest one available. It was certainly time for an upgrade! And I am forever grateful to Loren Martin, Joerns Healthcare, and Diversicare for their compassion, which made this transfer change possible.

I originally wanted this chapter to focus only on the best caregivers—my most loyal, talented, caring employees for whom I have the utmost gratitude. However, since they know who they are, I was instead prompted to share a warning to all who rely on this service—learn from my mistakes.

I had the opportunity to meet a young paraplegic recently, and I found myself explaining the importance of an employee handbook. "Get things in writing." This young woman had her spinal cord removed surgically due to a cancerous tumor, and she found the first few months with caregivers to be extremely disappointing. I hope by sharing what I learned of this job as "boss" of my cares, I have empowered her to communicate her expectations and retain only the best workers. It's not a flawless system, but it works best when established standards are clear.

Doug occasionally reminds me that training and scheduling caregivers is essentially a second job, and it's difficult at times. But over the years, I have concluded that my system works well for me. Every new caregiver hears me say, "You are my hands." If they understand this, they begin to comprehend the model of team effort it takes to bring quality and productivity to our lives. And I truly mean "our lives." This is a unique job. Not many hear the call to do it. I hope each and every caregiver feels tremendous reward from helping me accomplish my daily goals for a purpose-filled life.

CHAPTER SEVENTEEN

PURPOSE IN THE MOST UNEXPECTED PLACES

O NE LESSON I CANNOT turn away from—something perhaps a quadri-plegic learns more deeply in life than an able-bodied person—is that relationships matter. Spinal cord injury or not, we need each other. My life was made better by a tragedy; my last step backward brought me gifts that I believe would have been overlooked, completely missed, had I not been brought to an abrupt stop that said, "Hey, pay attention!"

When I left the Old Tasha on that concrete theater floor so many years ago, I began a rebirth. The New Tasha Schuh learned to ask for help—God's help, as well as help from the people He put in my path. Family, friends, medical experts, caregivers, church members, coworkers—suddenly everyone mattered. The next move forward could not have occurred without them.

I'd like to think that the Old Tasha Schuh would have held every human being in high esteem as she matured throughout life, but my disability truly made me pause and think about others more deeply. Aren't we here on this earthbound journey to learn to love, to give of ourselves to each other? Don't we serve Jesus best by serving those who truly need us?

For a time, I feared I had lost my ability to not only serve myself, but others, too. Yet no lesson is more absolute than this: giving results in getting. The rewards we experience when we give unselfishly to others are endless or, like the credit card slogan says, priceless. Yet knowing our gifts—the talents we possess that benefit others—takes some searching. And this search seems to be a big part of the journey God asks us to take.

It took some time for me to realize that when I ask others for their gifts—when I need their help and support—they benefit in return. And when I give of myself, when I express gratitude, when I show love for those I encounter, and when—more recently, as a writer and national speaker—I share my lessons from confronting this challenging way of life, I too receive by knowing I help others. People who experience a drastic change in what they expected life to bring them—well, these people need me. They need my gift of hope. I have come to the profound realization that through me, others feel inspired to overcome whatever boundaries they may feel, whatever disappointments they fear have altered their lives forever. I am living proof that, although not easy, life can and will go on, and it can be wonderful—maybe even better than expected!

In the early chapters of the New Tasha Schuh, although I hoped I had something to share with others, I feared I had little to offer this world. I "stuffed" that feeling, but it was always present.

I have to ask people for everything. I can't roll over in bed; I can't use the bathroom or shower alone; I can't dress myself; I can't get situated in my wheelchair. I can do none of this without the assistance of others.

Clear witness to my transformation came with time and faith. And my hope is, in reading my books, hearing my presentations, and receiving my email updates, people realize that this transformation can happen to everyone. Not a single person can experience life on this planet without loving, connecting, and needing others. The most talented, independent, able-bodied people must learn this lesson, too. Purposefully choosing to be around people who lift us in life—people who support us and permit us to be who we are destined to be—will prove to be the most valuable decisions we make in this time on earth.

I have come to call this my PITCrew—my posse, my team, my closest and most trusted loved ones. Fans of NASCAR know that a pit stop is when a racer pulls over to an area called "the pit" for a tire change, refueling, mechanical adjustments, or anything else that the crew can do to support the driver's goal: a successful finish! The driver cannot win without this team.

Doug and I have seen the power of a pit crew on the racetrack, and we want to take that energy and apply it across the country. It's more than a metaphor. It's the power which comes when people share their goals for a good life, then raise their checkered flag while they gather their crew and ultimately celebrate in the winner's circle—not just once, but over and over as we face the test of life.

Doug and I launched the PITCrew Movement as our business began to take new form. Our marriage has strengthened our business, Tasha Schuh Inspirations, just as our business has strengthened our marriage—a point this final chapter will drive home. However, it took a tragedy to really spark the full vision of the PITCrew Movement. It took a friend from the past, a classmate to the Old Tasha, to see exactly why this movement was so needed in our world.

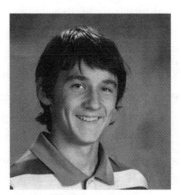

Logan Hinrichs at age 14.

In 2014, a friend from high school, Emmy, lost her teenage son to every parent's worst fear—suicide. On December 14, 2014, at the age of fourteen, Logan Hinrichs, a middle school student from Red Wing, Minnesota, took his own life. He never said, "I'm depressed." He wasn't a child who left "warning signs," which are often identified in suicide-prevention training. But there's no doubt he was hurting. Two days after his mom's birthday, and just hours after he and his mom sang along to the radio while they drove down the road, Logan ended his life.

If it hadn't been for a five-page note found on his cell phone, Emmy wouldn't have believed it. The only thing that seemed odd for this happy, easy-to-raise child was a bit of trouble at school just weeks prior to his death. Logan had gotten into a fight with a classmate—something this gentle boy had never experienced. Both boys involved were suspended. Logan got a regular out-of-school suspension; the other boy served an in-school suspension. Logan was upset because this was his first offense, and the other boy had many other past offenses. The whole thing was so out of character for Logan. But he served his punishment and went back to school.

Emmy wondered if this incident triggered something deep and painful for Logan. But the suicide note did not explicitly say this event had anything to do with Logan's decision to take his life. Emmy made sure the other boy was aware of this. Logan never stated a clear answer as to who or what was the reasoning for his decision. Logan's note left things unclear, yet one thing was sure: Logan's writings were beyond his age, so deep, so mature. Clearly, he had concerns about the purpose of his life and the path for his future.

Nothing will bring back her child. But Emmy has courageously agreed to share Logan's story and to allow me to use this tragic outcome to show just how great a need there is for the world to connect and support each other.

I had only met Logan a couple times, but he always stood out as such a sweet, confident, handsome boy. When I found out that he had ended his life, I could not believe it. I had officiated the wedding of Emmy and Luke—a very loving stepdad to Logan—a couple years earlier. Anticipating many students at the funeral, Emmy and Luke asked me to be a part of the eulogy and to share my story in hopes that this might help prevent another tragedy among young listeners. Despite all of her pain, Emmy was thinking of others. She wanted them to know that ending it all was not the answer—that Logan should have reached out for help.

Speaking at Logan's funeral was one of the hardest things I've ever had to do. I had cried uncontrollably since I first heard the news, and I felt I would not be able to find my voice. With prayers for strength, I pulled it together, but I knew that I never wanted to do something like this ever again. Logan was fourteen years old, and he had such a bright future in front of him! Nothing is more tragic to me than an unnecessary loss of young life.

Afterward, I started hearing the statistics on youth and those who take their own lives. Statistics like: suicide is the second-leading cause of death among young people every year. As numbers unfolded, I began to read more stories of kids taking their lives—even as young as eight years old! Names and faces replaced statistics. I knew that we needed to do something. Doug and I seemed to have the same thought simultaneously: *We cannot sit back and watch this continue without taking some kind of action.*

Hence, the PITCrew Movement was born. In researching suicide, we found the most unifying theme to be loneliness. They feel that no one cares about them, and they just want the pain to stop.

I knew this feeling. It was painful to take a step back there—back to the hospital room where I faced the tragic loss of mobility and struggled to heal, to breathe, and to say goodbye to a body I no longer had full control over. I knew what it felt like to wish I had died on the concrete floor.

However, I also knew the joy in fighting the despair embedded in such loss. I knew the exhilaration that came from winning a battle to overcome dread and loss while learning to move forward. Empathy is powerful. After a lot of searching, Doug and I knew one thing—the PITCrew Movement had to connect people.

At the darkest moment, every single human being in this world must know there is someone to go to—someone to trust. By design, the PITCrew needed to address this. We had to strive to eliminate suicide as an option to despair.

Many months later, clarity has come to our mission: first and foremost, prevention. We intend to build trust by instructing others on how to create their own PITCrew. This is our small, handpicked group of trusted individuals who will help and encourage us. In our darkest times and even in our greatest moments of joy, we each need our own team. We need those people who will provide support without judgment. We need unconditional love.

This mission, this PITCrew Movement, will strengthen the human experience and help stop the needless suffering that others do alone. We hope everyone believes us when we say, the process is sheer joy! Establishing your PITCrew is a blast! How often do you think about creating a list of the best people in your life? Think of the trust and good feeling gained by telling someone he or she is on your list!

An established PITCrew network might never have to be used in a dire situation. The network might just be a fun what-if, spreading friendship and reminding others how much they are loved, respected, and needed in others' lives and in this world. But when your life becomes challenging, ask yourself, in that moment, *Who are the people I can count on for help? Can I name them?*

If so, that's great. If not, start thinking about the people you spend time with; are they of the caliber needed to lift and encourage you to be the best person you can be? Creating your PITCrew list just might be the step you need to turn some negative things around, filling your life with people who lift you up, not pull you down.

People ask me, "Isn't this depressing for you? Wouldn't you rather focus on the joys of your successes?" My answer is, "I do." Success comes as we do this for Logan. Joy comes as we help his family members who question what went wrong. And joy also comes when a teenager approaches us after a school talk and shares how they were helped by this message—how they were struggling and contemplating their next move forward.

I pursue the PITCrew Movement so that the pain of loneliness and alienation can stop, so that the joy I've experienced from coming out of the darkness of the Sheldon Theater basement, into the light of faith, friendship, and family, can flourish. Nothing would give me greater joy than to know that I helped prevent another tragic loss from suicide.

Emmy agrees wholeheartedly. As hard as it is to persevere after the loss of Logan, Emmy gave me permission to talk about her son at schools, in presentations—wherever the PITCrew Movement has the potential to change lives. She wants us to flip an attitude of despair into a dream of hope.

For me, the PITCrew has a relationship of mutual membership. I have my crew members, and I also have membership on their PITCrew. We need each other and must function in a reciprocal way.

My PITCrew starts with my family—those who believed in me from the start, cheered me on in the darkest moments, and said they wouldn't let me die without a fight. For me, this also includes the friends and care-givers, whose gifts are twofold. They serve me with kindness and patience but also possess the characteristics that every best friend loves: a sense of humor, a secret bond, and an empathetic ear. In return, these people have my unconditional love and respect.

My PITCrew also includes my business team. Rachel is no longer my massage therapist but a talented contributing member of this movement. Her marketing expertise sprang us into action—on our website, through our presentation literature, and via social media—in creative ways that only she could generate. My niece Isabel, whose college experience is just beginning, supports Rachel's work with a marketing eye that allows the PITCrew Movement to be relevant to people her age. Her input has been essential, especially with style and design ideas that Doug and I simply don't have the knack for. Thankfully, technology will make it possible for this to continue from her new college home.

I am anticipating that my other nieces, Anna and Ella, will join my care-giver team as they become old enough to help. Yet—whether they work for me or not—my nieces and my nephews, Cameron and Connor, can count on me to be a member of their PITCrew as they seek their independence in this ever-changing world.

My PITCrew would not be complete without Doug—my closest con-fidant in life. Doug takes on a unique and large role in my personal and professional life, and it grows naturally every year. My world has changed so dramatically because he came into it. I am a better, more loving, more complete Tasha Schuh because Doug Michaels felt compelled to join me on my journey—to add me to his own PITCrew membership.

Throughout the course of this book, I am sure every reader has noted how many things Doug Michaels does in a given day. I laugh when I think of the criticism that was overheard when Doug left his meteorology job to manage my business. Some believed he was taking the easy route—as if he could live off of my growing business and not have to engage in it. In reality, when Doug agreed to take this job, neither of us knew how extensive this position would be. But success breeds growth in business. And as Doug has helped me grow the business, his responsibilities have grown exponentially.

In the military, the pit crew chief observes and maintains an aircraft or a ship. In NASCAR, the pit crew chief is more like the manager of all crew members involved, including the driver and the auto mechanics crew. I like the analogy of manager best because it nails the fact that Doug has eyes on every aspect of our home and business. Clearly, this is a manager who also must confront the demands of a CEO wife while maintaining a level of professionalism with me.

Doug's management skills have helped me reach more people than I ever dreamed possible simply because he is so gifted at networking. My full calendar schedule exists because Doug initiates contacts and follows up on these initial calls. He perseveres and delivers what clients want and expect. In addition, Doug is also calling new contacts at schools and businesses that may have speaker needs. This results in many hours on the phone and creates future work not just for me, the presenter, but also for the PITCrew chief, who must manage all of this.

Last winter, our PITCrew Club vision got its chance. We were asked to present after a tragic chain of events occurred in the Hammond, Wisconsin, community. St. Croix Central High School partnered with us after losing four teenagers to suicide within three years. The pain of loss was compounded by the fear that an epidemic could cause more students to consider this tragic option. Our experience with Hammond's students and staff clinched our belief that the PITCrew Movement was a highly effective approach to mental-health awareness and suicide prevention. Such a caring and close-knit community should not have loss like this.

Speaking at St. Croix Central High School where we piloted the PITCrew Club.

We piloted the PITCrew Club with St. Croix Central volunteer students. These students came forward to initiate involvement because they either struggled with mental illness themselves or felt compelled to help others who grapple with depression or thoughts of suicide. In five short months, starting in January 2017, we accomplished so much in our monthly meetings before school let out for summer break. One of those things included a Suicide Prevention Week with activities that went beyond the typical prevention program and included these highlights:

1. Wearing a yellow ribbon to demonstrate support and concern
2. Creating and distributing "Kindness Counts" cards to remind students how tragedy can be prevented if students show genuine kindness to others
3. A balloon release in memory of those who have attempted or have taken their lives by suicide

This powerful experience led many students to indicate for the first time that they had been struggling with thoughts of suicide. The guidance counselors later informed us that students filtered in and out of their office throughout the week—seeking help, wanting to talk, hoping to find a compassionate ear. The counselors thought, *Bingo—this is the very first step in prevention! This is why we are doing what we are doing!*

The PITCrew Movement works because at its core, it digs deeper than a typical suicide prevention program. It inspires all participants to build their PITCrew team, a relationship-building concept that leads to a purpose-driven life. I firmly believe suicide will diminish if people become more purposefully engaged in life's goals, as I have.

You can imagine how thrilled I was when Emmy agreed to join us one day—to speak, if only briefly, about Logan and her desire to prevent this tragedy from happening again. Her courage in speaking directly for Logan to the St. Croix Central students empowered her as well as every person listening that day. With no training and possessing the common aversion to public speaking, Emmy faced her fears and shared Logan's story so eloquently. Every listener was moved by her motivation to talk about the hardest thing she has faced in her life.

Emmy's willingness to address a gym full of strangers and then challenge all of them to do their best to prevent others from falling to the same despair as Logan—well, I cannot overstate the impact this had on people.

Doug's commitment to all of this is essential to my purpose. As my PITCrew chief, he recently discovered a program for us to join that will help in our mission to speak at more schools and address what the Center for Disease Control identifies as the second-leading cause of death among youth ages ten to twenty-four. Doug and I are engrossed in a continuing education study, preparing us for our PITCrew movement directly focused on schools. Since there is no certification program for this, Doug's commitment to self-education fuels our next step. Meanwhile, I continue to create and tweak my presentations to stress the importance of mental health awareness and suicide prevention everywhere we speak.

Logistics for something like our PITCrew Club Pilot Program in the Hammond community were challenging, yet so rewarding. We will follow up throughout the school year with the team of youth who we are planning to train as leaders in this local program. Can you imagine when an event takes place over a thousand miles away from our home and office? With social media and my PITCrew team behind me, this and more is possible.

Doug is prepared for the PITCrew Movement growth we anticipate this year. In charge of logistics for each professional engagement, he is the reason that everything goes so smoothly. I also love that Doug now introduces me at every event.

As we travel, the PITCrew will ebb and flow, so my PITCrew Chief must also be trusting of the people who come in and out of my world. I recommend that everybody choose a leader for their list, realizing that this individual can change over time. Identify your PITCrew chief, and choose someone who will accept the many relationships you make along life's journey.

My PITCrew is a living, breathing, evolving chain of connections I make in life. It is not exclusive. It can't be a closed final roster. I must be watchful for new connections all of the time. I might miss some of the most influential, life-changing of God's people if I put my van in park for too long.

Take for example the influence a former neighbor continues to have on my life. No day goes by without me speaking to or at least thinking of him. I can't pull out of my driveway and exit my neighborhood—a place he hasn't lived for years—without recalling the time he spent living a few doors down from me. And although he has left this earth for another world—Heaven, assuredly—TJ Helgeson has left an indelible mark on my soul for all he endured, for all of the courage he showed in his life. He was an unforeseen addition to my PITCrew, but thank God I was attentive to the impact such an unexpected hero would have in my life.

I think my tribute to TJ—a message written on my website soon after cancer took him from his beautiful family—says it best. My reaction, upon hearing that TJ lost his life after fighting a miserable disease with the courage only a loving husband and father knows, is reprinted here:

In this journey called life, there are people who enter your path, and after doing so, they impact you so much that you will never be the same. For me, one of those people was TJ Helgeson.

I met TJ in 2009 after he began dating my neighbor Renee. Renee and I had become friends after she moved into her new home in 2008. We were the only single women in our neighborhood, so we hit it off after meeting.

I remember Renee telling me how she met TJ and how she was excited for me to meet him. Shortly after that, I was introduced to him. We quickly found out what a small world it was as I knew his uncle and had been good friends with him and his wife for a couple of years prior to meeting TJ.

In the busyness of life, we would see each other in passing, and they would stop over to my house every so often. One time they stopped over to introduce their new dog, Mya, a black lab–husky mix. I tried to warn them as they entered the house with their proud new puppy, but before I could say anything, my cat Lily jumped up to show this dog whose house this was and who was in control. Thankfully, Lily's front paws are declawed, so she did not hurt Mya. It was a funny sight to see this little cat thinking that she was bigger than a dog the size of a lab!

It was the following spring when I heard the news that TJ had been diagnosed with a rare form of leukemia. I instantly began following his CaringBridge page. Every time I received a notification, I would read it immediately. I would pray for him multiple times a day and was so encouraged by his faith, his positive attitude, and his courage. When reading his journal entries, I could see the pain that he was going through; yet his determination to overcome was bigger than the cancer.

During this time I was going through some of my own struggles. I had recently been in a relationship that ended badly, which was very difficult for me. Shortly after that, I had developed a skin sore for which doctors told me I would need to be in bed until it healed. A year before my Gillette Hospital surgery, I would spend approximately two and a half months in bed, flat on my back at home. There were days that were difficult and frustrating, and yet I would think of all TJ was going through. If he could do it, so could I.

I was thankful that I could be at home, whereas TJ was forced to stay in the hospital away from germs because his immune system was so weak. I was not sick or nauseous; TJ was dealing with routine vomiting and skin sores that covered the inside of his mouth and throat. After he came home from the hospital, I would look down the street at their house from my big bedroom window, and remind myself how fortunate I was. I remembered TJ, and thus made a daily decision to be thankful for where I was, even though it was less than ideal. I continued reading his journal entries and could not wait to tell him how much he inspired me during this time.

After he was home and in remission, we decided to meet and hang out. I was so excited to tell him how he had helped me during my time of being laid up in bed, but before I could get the words out, he began telling me how much I inspired him when he was going through his recovery, after coming home from the hospital. His words tell it best from his journal entries on his CaringBridge site:

It was at this same time when I barely had enough energy to scrape myself out of bed to walk to the bathroom. Doctors told me it would be beneficial to my recovery if I pushed myself within reason. Taking small walks was the best thing I could do to prevent lung infections, etc. It was the absolute last thing I wanted to do. I was feeling sorry for myself and had every excuse in the book not to go and push myself. I remember on many occasions walking past my front door and looking out the window. What did I see? I saw Tasha's house. I froze and would think to myself . . . Tasha would give anything to be able to stand from her wheelchair and walk around the block. And here I am, standing on able-legs and feeling sorry for myself. I looked at life from Tasha's PERSPECTIVE for a change. It was shortly thereafter I found myself tying my shoes, putting on a jacket, my mask, and making the slowest walk ever to the end of my road.

We realized in these moments that without knowing it, we had helped each other through a very difficult time. Looking at life through a different lens, another person's perspective, gave us both strength to persevere and to not give up.

Since that time in 2011, TJ continued to be my inspiration. After their marriage, I had the privilege of watching him and Renee become parents—first to their son, Kadyn, and then, last September, their daughter Blakely. Witnessing TJ go back to work, even though it was hard getting his energy back, motivated me to give my best effort every day. I was truly devastated and heartbroken when I received the CaringBridge notification titled "5 Year Relapse." I read the journal entry that said the cancer was back and no longer curable; he was going home to make the most of his last days.

TJ lost his battle to cancer and went to heaven on July 6, 2016. He was only thirty-two years old. Today I see him as my hero. TJ has influenced my life in so many ways through his struggles, love of life, and determination. I will never forget him, and plan on taking his story with me as I travel and speak. His legacy will live on, and I am determined that the world will know who he was. Even though he isn't able to speak and share his story now, I am hoping that my words can tell of his passion and zeal for life, and just maybe help others to be thankful for each day, and to live life to the fullest.

Whether we know it or not, we all have influence. Every interaction that we have is either positive or negative—there is no neutral. When I leave this earth I want to be remembered in the same way I remember TJ today . . . that we changed lives for the better, and we made a positive difference. And so I ask you today, how are you impacting and influencing lives for the better? What legacy will you leave on this earth when you are no longer here? What can you change in your life that will, in turn, influence others and help them to live life to the fullest?

I want to leave you today with some of the words that TJ wrote in his journals on CaringBridge; they not only impacted me but I believe will impact you as well!

"The fun that I had this weekend was just a great reminder that within my personal 'to do' list will have a task that reads, 'Make a memory'. How often a person decides to do this task is their decision, but I know after what I have experienced this past year, it will be much more frequent on my list. We can't remember all of life's tasks but we can remember life's memories."

To live like you are dying is to realize how rich we all really are, despite the few things we possess or how thin our wallets might be. It is making each day the best for ourselves and more importantly for everyone around us. Offer a smile, a helping hand, a listening ear, whatever it is you have to offer, because when you are faced with a fight for your life, these are the things you will be remembered by.

Thank you TJ for all that you gave me . . . I know I will see you again!

The strength of TJ Helgeson will inspire me forever.

Courage comes at unexpected times. I watched TJ confront all of the unknowns while enduring two battles with cancer. TJ overcame fear beyond comprehension . . . enough to marry the love of his life while engulfed in treatment, enough to tackle the hurdles of fatherhood, enough to leave two beautiful children as his legacy for Renee.

I often ask myself, *What if TJ could have one more day? What would he do? How would he spend it?* How often we miss the opportunity for joy and waste precious moments over insecurities and fear that do nothing but steal time.

Where are you allowing fear of failure—the fear of the future—to hold you back from living the dreams that live inside you? I almost missed out on the best gift that God has given me. I almost missed meeting Doug Michaels. I almost let fear stop me from dating. I was so afraid to get close enough to someone, out of fear that he would reject the real me—the New Tasha Schuh. I now see the power of courage that led me to the man of my dreams.

I am not regretful that I waited for someone who was clearly the best man for me. However, fear should not take us out of the search for full meaning and the potential to experience all that God intends. I am so thankful that He led me to take my next move forward, to continue this joy-filled life with new adventures and experiences that come with knowing the best is yet to come. Faith is knowing this will happen when we believe it and live it. A healthy dose of hope will help us discover that, no matter how dark, how grueling, how frightening life seems to be, we all have the courage to conquer our fears. And, with it, the sensitive hearts of people who are hurting, like Logan, will find strength to carry on.

We do not know what mysteries lie before us. Isn't that the definition of faith—resilience in the face of uncertainty? I do not wish to spend much time thinking about what I might have missed had I given up or had I settled for a solitary life. I definitely have learned that none of us knows when something or someone will change our lives forever. I reflect just enough to say, "Whew—that was a close call." I think back just enough to feel gratitude for all that Doug has brought to my life. I continue to believe the best is yet to come. And if God can top what I've experienced already,

I will surely go down in history as the happiest woman ever. Not a bad legacy for a girl who temporarily lost it all.

Tasha and Doug visited the Wisconsin State Capitol, in Madison to accept the Hometown Hero Award, 2017. Tasha was nominated by Wisconsin State Assembly member Warren Petryk.

ACKNOWLEDGMENTS

THERE ARE CERTAIN PEOPLE that I must thank for their support throughout this project. Without them, this book would not exist.

First, to Doug. In these few years of being married to you, I have learned so much about love, trust, and how wonderful life can be with an amazing partner. Thank you for being the remarkable husband, lover, and friend that you are.

To all my wonderful family and friends—you have been here for me, believed in me, encouraged me, supported me in difficult decisions, and helped me more than you'll ever know. You have helped shape me into the person that I am today, so that I could be a living example of hope and perseverance.

Jan Pavloski, who has spent hours upon hours sacrificing so much in putting this book together. It was such a joy working with you again and I'm so thankful for you! You have been blessed with such amazing abilities and creativity, which made this project flow and come together so perfectly. Your patience and your fun-loving attitude made this project so much fun to work on and would've never happened without you.

Ashlee Lundvall, this book would be incomplete without your input and help. Thank you for offering your knowledge and experience to make this book the best that it can be.

Finally, I lift this project up to God, who never lets me stay in my comfort zone. He always provides courage and faith for me to see His amazing plan unfold. Because I know He's with me, I am excited to see all the surprises He still has in store.

BOOK CLUB QUESTIONS

1. Although a reader doesn't need to have read Tasha's first memoir in order to understand this one, what essentials about her accident are important to fully appreciate this book?

2. Tasha Schuh seems very courageous for someone facing daily living obstacles to her mobility. What is it in her that seems to drive her most? Faith? Curiosity? A need to help others? All of the above?

3. Although Tasha is often fearless, what was one fear that kept her from dating? Do you think she was wise to be so cautious? Explain.

4. Online dating is popular and a socially acceptable way of meeting people today. Do you think Tasha's experience is common? Would you recommend it to your best friend as a means of meeting Mr. or Ms. Right?

5. Memories of the Old Tasha come back at times for her. What would you/do you miss the most regarding the loss of mobility? How would/have your loved ones been affected because of mobility issues in your life?

6. Doug seems very attentive and caring from the very beginning of their relationship. What were the first clues that he was perhaps different than most men regarding Tasha's paralysis? What were the first signs that he was a committed partner in this relationship?

7. Despite the joy and fun in their early days as a couple, both Tasha and Doug definitely consider marriage a lifelong commitment to be taken seriously. What things impress you regarding their efforts to plan for a lasting marriage? Should everyone take such steps in preparing for this commitment?

8. Tasha believes that part of what attracted Doug to her was her independent nature. List the things Tasha seems to have conquered before meeting Doug—things which make him almost forget that she is disabled.

9. Why do you think the turnout for Tasha's wedding was so great? What made this such a big event for friends, family, even acquaintances?

10. Before reading Tasha's book, what stereotypes did you believe about people with disabilities? Were any of them regarding sexuality? In your mind, what myths or stereotypes have been dispelled after reading this book?

11. What elements must be present for a couple to successfully work together in their careers? What do Tasha and Doug do to make this blur between home and work successful?

12. Do you agree with Tasha's choice to hire and essentially be the boss of her caregivers? Would you do things the same way? Differently? Explain.

13. Do you agree with Tasha's belief that family should not work as regular caregiving staff? Explain.

14. Who would you pick for your PITCrew Team? What makes Doug a primary member of Tasha's team—in other words, her PITCrew Chief? Who would be your chief? Explain.

15. What aspects of the PITCrew Movement do you like best? What would you add or change if you had the chance to get involved?

16. Do you think Tasha has a unique perspective on issues like suicide prevention? Why?

17. TJ Helgeson made a lasting impression on Tasha and Doug. Name one person no longer in your life who can still influence you in a positive way. How is this "absent" PITCrew member still present? Why still so important?

18. Name one person you know who would benefit from reading Tasha's story. Explain why.

BIBLIOGRAPHY

Brown, Brené. *The Gifts of Imperfection: Let Go of Who You Think You're Supposed to Be and Embrace Who You Are.* Center City, MN: Hazelden, 2010.

Chapman, Gary. *The Five Love Languages.* 2015. http://www.5lovelanguages.com/

Eareckson Tada, Joni. *Choices, Changes.* Grand Rapids, MI: Zondervan, 1986.

Feeling Your Way: *Relationships and Sexuality after Spinal Cord Injury.* Rochester, MN: Mayo Foundation for Medical Education and Research, 2012. DVD.

Gregoire, Sheila Wray. *The Good Girl's Guide to Great Sex.* Grand Rapids, MI: Zondervan, 2012.

Lewis, C. S. *The Four Loves.* San Francisco: HarperOne, 2017.

Moore, Beth. *So Long, Insecurity: You've been a Bad Friend to Us.* Carol Stream, IL: Tyndale House, 2010.

"Spinal Cord Injury: Complications," Mayo Foundation for Medical Education and Research. 1998-2017. http://www.mayoclinic.org/diseases-conditions spinal-cord- injury/basics/complications/con-20023837

Looking for a Speaker?
Your next event needs Tasha!

Speaker, Author & Founder of the PITCrew

Tasha brings...

Relevant Message - Audience connection for all ages. Tasha blends goals, passion and power that will leave everyone wanting to hear more.

Unique Story - Paralyzed for over half her life, Tasha's story creates inspiration and fresh perspective.

Experience - Beginning her speaking career in 2007, Tasha knows how to impact audiences of every size.

Ease & Enjoyment - Creating a five star experience for your group, Tasha will ensure your event goals are achieved.

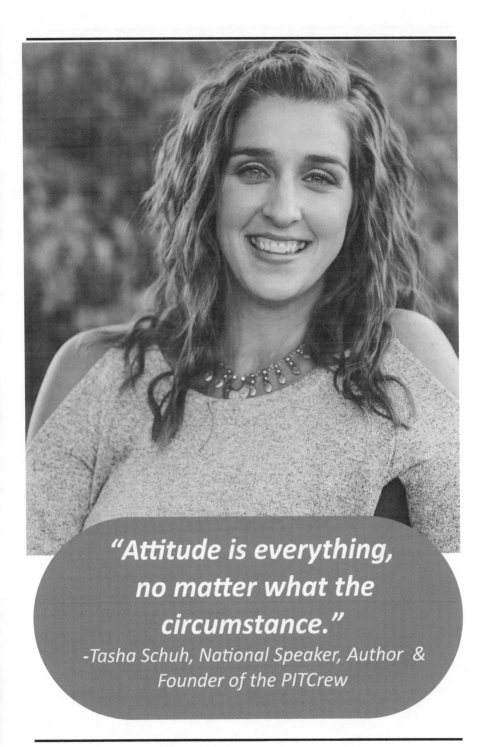

"Attitude is everything,
no matter what the
circumstance."

-Tasha Schuh, National Speaker, Author &
Founder of the PITCrew

TOGETHER WE CAN FINISH STRONG

Be A Part of Something Bigger...

The PITCrew was created by Tasha to help others gain a better understanding of how to 'Enjoy Their Ride' wherever they might be within their lives.

The PITCrew encourages us to:

• Support others to the best of our ability

• Ask for help when needed

• Accept imperfections and appreciate our differences

• Help each other move forward

• Celebrate successes and *Finish Strong*

In schools, PITCrew tackles the epidemics of bullying and suicide. In the business community, PITCrew encourages teamwork and accelerating the momentum needed to reach the common goal.

Join the Movement.

Join the PITCrew!

WWW.TASHASCHUH.COM/PITCREW